I loved
receiving these books,

Ethel Tillinghast

AMERICAN
HERITAGE

December 1967 · Volume XIX, Number 1

Essay: What Is Important in History? *By* MORRIS BISHOP

An academic eavesdropper, bugging college classrooms, would hear endlessly repeated the lecturer's phrase "a matter of the utmost importance is ..." The conclusion of the sentence, accompanied by a squeak of chalk, might be almost anything: "the Occasional Conformity Act of 1711," or "the Pragmatic Sanction of 1713," or "the Molasses Act of 1733." The cultural spy would observe the forward quarter of the class eagerly noting down what sounds like an examination question of the utmost importance, while the rearward three quarters, asprawl and aslump, indicate in every limb that the matter is of no importance at all. The teacher is mistaken, or possibly lying. If his pronouncement were of actual importance, his hearers would rouse, gape, cry approval, or protest. The teacher should properly qualify his statement to read, "A matter of the utmost importance to me personally is this or that," or, "A matter of the utmost importance to those who wish to get a good grade in the course is..." The teacher might in his gloomier moments amplify his reservations; he might ask himself what, if anything, is important in history.

It would seem that we have a simple and incontrovertible means of recognizing the important: it is interesting. But historians have been impelled to introduce a contrary principle. Honoring patient industry, they praise the researcher who has read through the English Court of Chancery records, or a mountain of French provincial archives, or the ledgers of a thousand early ironmongers in Oklahoma. This is splendid, of course; the researchers deserve all the praise they get, and more. However, they are applauded not because their work is interesting but because it is uninteresting. They are rewarded for their endurance in the study of the insignificant. Let us give them a great big hand instead of reading the massive volumes that result from their labors.

The exaltation of the unimportant is promoted by the value system of college teaching. The historian is pulled and pushed into publication. He is pulled by his desire to give the scholarly world something new, or something old that has been forgotten, even though justly forgotten. He longs to resurrect a skeleton and clack its bones together until he lets go and it relapses into its comfortable grave. At the same time, the historian is pushed by the academic demand that he publish for promotion, for the attainment of Tenure, that blissful state in which he need never again publish anything. So, until Tenure enfolds him, and sometimes after, he publishes.

In a recent issue of the *American Historical Review* I count critical reviews of 232 books and noncritical notices of 270 more. I do not number microfilms and the list of learned periodical articles, which outrun my ability to count. Many of these studies look interesting to me; I am sure that all of them are interesting, and hence important, to some subscribers to the *Review.* Long-felt wants are no doubt filled by *Thucydides and the Politics of Bipolarity,* by *The Council of Chalcedon and the Armenian Church,* by *Ancient Petitions Relating to Northumberland,* by *English Land Measuring to 1800,* by *Struktur und Funktion der "KPD-Opposition"* (*KPO*). But these are specialized importances; I am concerned rather with Importance in the large sense, Importance for the nonprofessional reader, who has the blessed privilege of stopping when he is bored.

If one examines a set of current historical textbooks, one sees that their authors agree pretty closely on what is important. In medieval history, for instance, ample space is always allotted to feudalism. It must be defined, analyzed, distinguished from the manorial system, and pursued through periods of dominance and decline. The student must be thoroughly instructed on feudal land tenure in various countries and on the forces at work to transform it into other systems of landholding. Again, the investiture controversy bulks large in every history of the Middle Ages. At issue was the question whether the pope or a monarch should invest a new bishop with his ring and crosier, symbols of his office. Again, or again again, every medieval history dwells at length on nominalism versus realism. Though of course *you* remember nominalism and realism, I may remind some less instructed reader of this essay that there are two attitudes toward universals, or generalized ideal classes. "The automobile" is a universal, whereas "my automobile" is a particular. The realists maintained that a universal is a reality, existing perfectly in God's mind. Not so, said the nominalists; universals are merely names, linguistic conveniences.

These three phenomena, or manifestations, or concretions—feudalism, the investiture controversy, the quarrel of universals—are all clearly important. In their own times they influenced men's lives and sometimes hastened their deaths. To some degree they have carried over into our own habits of thought. They are interesting—or at least interesting to those who are interested in this kind of thing.

But is their importance not perhaps overdone? Each of these subjects has produced a vast body of learned literature, filled with subtle argument, passion, and vituperation. One may wonder if the mass of commentary has not exalted the subjects above their intrinsic worth. One may wonder if, in modern parlance, there is not too much feedback in their circuits. One may even wonder if historical importance may not be defined as that which historians have liked to argue about.

If importance is what is of import, consequence, and value to me in my daily life, then feudalism, the investiture of bishops, nominalism and realism, all added together, are less important than the buttons on my coat and the zipper on my trousers. But what does history tell us about the button? Very little. The ancient Greeks and Romans had no buttons; they held themselves together with brooches and clasps and *fibulae,* safety pins. The button is not mentioned in the Bible;

hence some rigorous Amish still eschew the button, and there is, or was, a fundamentalist sect called "Hook-and-Eye Baptists." Up to the middle of the Middle Ages, Europeans fastened their cloaks and gowns at shoulder or breast with clasps or buckles, and tied their breeches with laces, thongs, or "points."

The button was apparently invented, like so much else, in China, with the linking of garments by a kind of toggle and with the application of frogs to silk to hold buttons and preserve buttonholes. The earliest reference that I have discovered to a button in Europe is in Robert de Clari's account of the coronation of Baldwin of Flanders as Emperor of the East, in Constantinople in the year 1204.

By the end of the thirteenth century there had been an explosion of buttons in western Europe, and they were standard equipment in the fourteenth. They were used for service and display; gentlemen wore a row of buttons on their sleeves, as we continue to do to show our respect for history.

I have dwelt at such length on the history of the button because no historian (apparently) has done so, and because its history seems to me perhaps as important as that of the royal crown or the papal tiara. Once history was chiefly military; then it became political, then economic and sociological. The history of ideas has its vogue, and so has the history of science and technology. The abundance and variety of histories suggests that there is no one measure of importance, but that one subject can be treated from many points of view. Everything is important to someone, somewhere, somewhen. Or so at least the historian hopes. Said Dr. Johnson, "All knowledge is of itself of some value. There is nothing so minute or inconsiderable that I would not rather know it than not. A man would not submit to learn to hem a ruffle, of his wife, or his wife's maid; but if a mere wish could attain it, he would rather wish to be able to hem a ruffle."

Much of history is hemming ruffles. But a ruffle well hemmed may be important, and not to the hemmer alone.

The historian wants to preserve everything in memory. He wants to

be useful, to do good. He points insistently to "the lessons of history." Few take his lessons seriously, except other historians. If the lessons of history were actually useful, our departments of history would be assailed by demands from mayors and congressmen asking history's solutions to their problems. The fire chief, on hearing an alarm, would hastily consult the History of Conflagrations. But fire chiefs, mayors, and congressmen use history only as an ornament to beautify or conceal their purpose. One of the rare examples in history of a ruler's serious appeal to history for guidance was that of Woodrow Wilson, himself a historian. He took a shipload of historians to Versailles in 1919 to make the treaty. And the Treaty of Versailles was rather worse than most treaties, in the judgment of later historians.

The lessons of history are as obscure and equivocal as the oracles at Delphi and Dodona. Its chief lesson is that it has no lessons. Its importance lies

only in itself. Its subject is all that man has done in past time. And past time is all time, for the present is only a knife-edge division between past and future. There is no present; we cannot be sure that there is any future. History, the entire past of mankind and of ourselves, envelops us. We cannot escape from history except into death or senility. If any spark of curiosity lives in us, we must be interested in history. When we lose our curiosity, the end is near.

But what is important in history? Everything is important, because everything touches us, at one remove or at a trillion. The life of an Egyptian slave, or of a Scythian chieftain, or of a potter in an Indian pueblo has infinitesimally affected our own lives, and may be ours again in imagination. Our imagination is our reality, and all that occupies it is important.

On the other hand, nothing is important, except our life and death, which are not very important either.

"As soon as I have made my Important Historic Statement, kindly put me down and get back in the fight, men. I think we're losing."

DRAWN FOR AMERICAN HERITAGE BY MICHAEL RAMUS

3

*As the lamp glow struggles against the misty darkness of
a frosty evening in the 1890's, Philadelphia's South Broad
Street seems to offer whichever we care to find—winter's-
night snugness or a gentle mood of urbane mystery.*

AMERICAN HERITAGE

The Magazine of History

SENIOR EDITOR
Bruce Catton

EDITOR
Oliver Jensen

MANAGING EDITOR
Robert L. Reynolds

ART DIRECTOR
Murray Belsky

ART EDITOR
Joan Paterson Kerr

ARTICLES EDITOR
E. M. Halliday

ASSOCIATE EDITORS
Robert S. Gallagher   David G. Lowe
Barbara Klaw   John L. Phillips
Douglas Tunstell

CONTRIBUTING EDITOR: Mary Cable

COPY EDITOR: Brenda Niemand

EDITORIAL ASSISTANTS
Mary Dawn Earley   Rosemary L. Klein
Mary A. Hawkins   Joanne Shapiro

PUBLISHER
Darby Perry

ADVISORY BOARD
Allan Nevins, *Chairman*
Carl Carmer   Louis C. Jones
Gerald Carson   Alvin M. Josephy, Jr.
Marshall B. Davidson   Howard H. Peckham
John A. Garraty   Francis S. Ronalds
Eric F. Goldman   S. K. Stevens

AMERICAN HERITAGE is published every two
months by American Heritage Publishing Co.,
Inc., 551 Fifth Avenue, New York, N.Y. 10017.

PRESIDENT
James Parton

CHAIRMAN, EDITORIAL COMMITTEE
Joseph J. Thorndike

EDITORIAL DIRECTOR, BOOK DIVISION
Richard M. Ketchum

SENIOR ART DIRECTOR
Irwin Glusker

Correspondence about subscriptions should be
sent to: American Heritage Subscription Office, 383 West Center Street, Marion, Ohio
43302. Single copies: $4.25. Annual subscrip-
tions: $16.50 in U.S. and Canada; $17.50 elsewhere. An annual Index of AMERICAN HERI-
TAGE is published in February, priced at $1.00.
AMERICAN HERITAGE will consider but assumes
no responsibility for unsolicited materials.
Title registered U.S. Patent Office. Second-
class postage paid at New York, N.Y., and
at additional mailing offices.

Sponsored by

American Association for State & Local History · Society of American Historians

CONTENTS *December, 1967 · Volume XIX, Number 1*

COVER: There have been many times in American maritime history when
vessels designed for the merchant marine have been pressed into military service.
The sturdy side-wheeler shown on our cover was built at Baltimore in 1836 for
commercial ventures, but during the Mexican War she was taken over by the
Army Quartermaster's Department and eventually had the honor of transporting
the American hero of that war, "Old Rough and Ready" Zachary Taylor, back
to his own country—on his way to the White House, as it turned out. An article
about the strangely ambivalent history of the American merchant marine,
together with a color portfolio of some of the beautiful ships that were once
our "pride of the seas," starts on page 64; the cover picture is from the India
House collection. *Back Cover:* A print from the collection of Carl H. Boehringer,
Tokyo, originally issued by the Japanese Ministry of Education around 1880,
explains to Japanese children some of the Yankee ingenuity of one Benjamin
Franklin, North American. The slightly mysterious Japanese caption is translated beneath the picture.

Greetin's, COUSIN

It was the first time in history to see what they lost in 1776. George hit it off like old friends; under the royal charm. Brewing was

A long line of nervous congressmen stood in the Capitol rotunda awaiting the arrival of someone of obviously high importance. Vice President John Nance Garner buzzed among the legislators trying to ease the tension with his famous stories. Toward the rear of the rotunda, members of the House tittered at Garner's jokes, while sober-faced senators critically eyed the antics of the Vice President. The audience pleased him. His jokes became less appropriate, the laughs grew louder, and the senators seemed less impressed. Then Garner walked over to the door and peered down the Capitol steps. Suddenly he turned back into the rotunda rasping, "The British are coming!"

Garner's sighting of the King and Queen of England was not as dramatic as "Cactus Jack" intimated. The royal invasion of the United States had begun two days before, on June 7, 1939, when a blue and silver streamlined train headed across the suspension bridge at Niagara Falls. Salutes boomed in the background as King George VI and his queen, Elizabeth, became the first reigning British monarchs ever to visit the United States. The twelve cars of the royal train passed over the bridge, and in less than five minutes the locomotive steamed into the brick and sandstone station.

The station was redolent of fresh paint. Decorations were scanty, but in a floodlight a small square of new crimson carpet protruded from the gloomy surroundings. There was no bunting—neither the budget of the New York Central system nor of the city of Niagara Falls could afford it—there were only small British and American flags crossed above the station door. "The simplicity of the scene" impressed an English correspondent; the aura of royalty impressed the American people.

The train braked to a stop, and more floodlights appeared. The red door of the observation car opened. His Most Excellent Majesty George VI, By the Grace of God, of Great Britain, Ireland, and of the British Dominions Beyond the Seas, King, Defender of the Faith, Emperor of India, stepped briskly from the car to the red carpet. His silver hair shining in the lights, the American Secretary of State, Cordell Hull, awaited the royal guests; Mrs. Hull stood at his side.

In his soft Tennessee drawl, Hull welcomed the royal couple and expressed hope that the visit would be a "thoroughly enjoyable one." The formalities over, they chatted for a few moments, then boarded the train. With a twenty-one-gun salute echoing in the station, the party began the overnight ride to Washington. As the train rolled into Buffalo, automobiles crammed the highways, their occupants seeking a glimpse of the King and Queen. One reporter remarked that if the train were on a campaign tour, "the King and Queen ought to carry Niagara County."

6

GEORGE

*that British sovereigns had come
and Franklin, Elizabeth and Eleanor,
even Texas congressmen melted
a crucial World War II alliance*

By PHILIP L. CANTELON

Beyond Hull's welcome, the floodlights, and the thundering salutes at the Suspension Bridge Station lay questions of international importance. The House of Commons had authorized conscription on April 27, 1939, and Germany and Italy announced a military and political alliance ten days later. Did the King and Great Britain seek assurances from the United States in the event of a world war, or something more? Was President Roosevelt leading the country into an unwanted alliance? Speaking with reporters early on the day of the King's arrival, Hull emphasized the effect the visit would have on nations that were "seriously threatened with chaos and anarchy" in international relations. He noted the closeness of American and British interests and referred to nations that were "disturbing the peace," thereby giving the trip a diplomatic tone. Some observers even speculated that Roosevelt had given Hull instructions to test public opinion on a prospective alliance. George VI had dropped a hint of British intentions while speaking in Banff, Alberta, a few days before, telling the gathering that "we" (the democracies) would "show them" (presumably the Axis nations). American reporters quickly interpreted this remark as pointing to an Anglo-American alliance. (The King's public-relations aides persuaded reporters not to disclose this incident, and when one American tried to telegraph the story to his paper, the Canadian communications office refused

to accept it.) As the royal train moved southward on the evening of June 9, Hull and the King discussed the "serious" conditions in Europe for more than a half hour. Perhaps clarification of the trip's purpose would come in Washington.

Preparations for the visit had long been in the making. Canadian Prime Minister Mackenzie King had been angling for a royal tour of North America since 1937. The idea intrigued Roosevelt, who, through his representative at the coronation of George VI in 1937, suggested a Washington visit. The new king was favorably inclined, but not until August, 1938, did arrangements for the trip to Canada begin to take form. Mackenzie King relayed the information to President Roosevelt.

At the height of the Munich crisis, in September, 1938, King George received a letter that Grace Tully, Roosevelt's private secretary, said was "as informal as any [Roosevelt] ever sent to an old friend." The letter contained an invitation for the royal family. "It would be an excellent thing for Anglo-American relations if you could visit the United States," Roosevelt wrote; ". . . if you bring either or both of the children with you they will also be very welcome, and I shall try to have one or two Roosevelts of approximately the same age to play with them!" The President knew the strains of a prolonged tour and the sweltering Washington weather. Might the King prefer

The progress of the royal couple was eagerly recorded by photographers. Above, the King shows the Queen the land of promise from the Canadian side of Niagara Falls; resplendent congressmen await them at the Capitol; the Queen weathers a sweltering garden party; at Mount Vernon, George VI honors the President who first urged caution in foreign alliances.

"three or four days of very simple country life" at Hyde Park? There would be "no formal entertainments" and it would provide "an opportunity to get a bit of rest and relaxation," he promised.

Roosevelt requested that talk of the visit remain outside normal diplomatic channels, and therefore secret, until plans matured. Discretion in the early stages might keep isolationist bloodhounds from sniffing out another "entangling alliance" and raising a howl against intrigue. The President asked his Ambassador to the Court of St. James's, Joseph P. Kennedy, to deliver the letter personally to the King. He happily delivered the invitation, but later became offended; since Roosevelt kept negotiations concerning the visit on a private rather than official basis, Kennedy soon found himself in the dark as to details. Feeling slighted by Roosevelt's methods, Kennedy angrily telegraphed Hull, complaining that "if I were not advised by the [British] Foreign Office, I would know nothing about the King's trip whatsoever. I hate to admit knowing nothing about it because that would seriously interfere, I imagine, with my prestige and contacts here." Roosevelt tried to soothe Kennedy. He explained to the Ambassador that the discussion "about the proposed visit of their Majesties next year is only in the preliminary stages and that, therefore, I am conducting it personally." Negotiations remained private.

Not until the settlement of the Czech question, which allowed Hitler to move into the Sudetenland but temporarily avoided war, did George VI answer Roosevelt's letter. On October 8 the King publicly announced his intention to visit Canada, and at the same time wrote to the President that he was looking forward to the trip, especially for its contributions "to the cordiality of the relations between our two countries." He noted that "we shall not be taking the children . . . as they are much too young for such a strenuous tour." Roosevelt replied on November 2, discussing in greater detail the projected visit. After talking with the British ambassador, Sir Ronald Lindsay, F. D. R. suggested a trip to Chicago and Washington, to New York City and the World's Fair, and to Hyde Park. He was not insistent about Chicago, but he did think the King "should go to a Joint Session of the Congress and say a few words of greeting." Concluding, he told the King he was happy "that Great Britain and the United States have been able to co-operate so effectively in the prevention of war— even though we cannot say that we are 'out of the woods' yet."

George VI agreed with Roosevelt's suggestions. His itinerary would include Washington, New York, and Hyde Park. The President was especially pleased that the King consented to visit Hyde Park. Mackenzie King would accompany his sovereign as Minister in Attendance. Mrs. Eleanor Roosevelt later wrote that her husband hoped their Majesties' visit "would create a bond of friendship between the people of the two countries." Despite the confident tone of his letter to the King, F. D. R. was convinced that war was just over the horizon and "wanted to make contacts with those he hoped would preserve and adhere to democracy and prove to be allies against fascism." Hyde Park would be the ideal setting for serious discussions, for Roosevelt felt that he knew people better once they had sampled the estate's charm. Talks there could be less tense and more personal. Washington and New York could attend to the formalities of the visit and satisfy public curiosity.

Thus in June, 1939, plans had become reality. As Hull was conversing with King George in the observation car, signals along the railroad flashed green, and the train continued steadily toward the American

The King admiringly inspected the Civilian Conservation Corps at a Virginia camp. In New York, where the royal welcome was extended by Mayor La Guardia (back to camera) and Governor Lehman, they were soon whisked out to the World's Fair for a painfully slow tour of the grounds. At Hyde Park the transportation, provided by F. D. R., was much more lively.

capital. George T. Summerlin, the chief of the State Department's Division of Protocol, worked with Colonel Edward J. Starling, chief of the Secret Service, to provide their Majesties adequate protection. Government agents checked every crossing, bridge, and culvert to insure a safe passage. But each inch of track from Niagara Falls to Washington could not be watched, so a pilot train preceded the royal special. If anarchists or the Irish Republican Army had mined the tracks, the King and Queen would still be safe. Newsmen riding in the pilot train were not enthusiastic about this arrangement. Somewhere in Pennsylvania, however, their locomotive developed a hot box and pulled off on a siding. The royal train rushed past, and the reporters arrived in Washington too late to witness the meeting of King George and President Roosevelt.

President and Mrs. Roosevelt and assorted notables had gathered in a special waiting room in Washington's gray and gold Union Station. This marked the first time that the President had greeted a foreign dignitary away from the White House door. Hull observed the proprieties: "Mr. President, I have the honor to present their Britannic Majesties." Smiling broadly, Roosevelt grasped the King's hand. "At last I greet you." The King replied, "It is indeed a pleasure for her Majesty and myself to be here." Immediately the Marine Corps Band struck up "God Save the King" (which they knew well enough as "My Country, 'Tis of Thee"), and followed with "The Star-Spangled Banner." Then F. D. R. escorted the King through the guard of honor toward waiting limousines. The King and President got in the first one, F. D. R. almost sitting on his top hat in the back seat. The Queen and Mrs. Roosevelt sat in the second car, and to a twenty-one-gun salute the motorcade began the slow drive to the White House.

Although Roosevelt believed the trip to Washington necessary, George VI, upon arrival, may have entertained second thoughts about its appropriateness. The warmth of the greeting at Union Station was nothing compared to the weather. The temperature soared to ninety-four degrees, and waves of heat rose from the street as the motorcade departed from the station. In their open car at the head of the parade, Roosevelt was almost suffocating in his cutaway, striped pants, and high hat, while the King, wearing the heavy full-dress uniform of an admiral of the fleet, came near to fainting from the heat—according to Grace Tully, he "could not have been more wretched had he been encased in a suit of armor."

Still, more than 600,000 people jammed Constitution Avenue to catch sight of royalty. They cheered wildly. Police, soldiers, and sailors, stationed every ten feet along the parade route, restrained the surging throng with difficulty. Ten Flying Fortresses and numerous fighter planes roared overhead, but they did not drown out the rumbling tanks and clattering cavalry in the parade, or the noisy crowd that fought for vantage points along its route. It appeared that all Washington had turned out. Although the visit was "unofficial," work stopped in the capital city. Schools were let out, government employees got the day off, shops closed, and even chain food stores shut down between eleven and one so their employees could ogle.

The procession turned onto Pennsylvania Avenue, where people had rented hotel rooms at exorbitant prices to get a clear view of the King and Queen. Guests jammed the windows. Unfortunately, to protect herself against the heat, Queen Elizabeth carried a parasol, mauve lined in green, which frustrated the window-wedgers above. Those on the searing pavement below were hardly better off. Stacked ten deep

in places, most of them strained mightily for only a momentary glimpse. Soldiers blocked the view of some, and ubiquitous Secret Service men trotted beside the cars, creating yet another obstruction. The crowd standing near Fourteenth Street and Pennsylvania edged away from the parade route when a light tank began to smoke, then stalled and burst into flames. Cavalrymen maneuvered their horses smugly around their disabled competition. But Americans had come to see royalty and they would not be denied. When Mrs. Roosevelt's waving blocked the crowd's view, a voice yelled, "Put your hand down! Let us see the Queen!"

There was little doubt in the crowd's mind; the Queen had stolen the show. Sitting on a specially constructed spring cushion, Elizabeth bowed continually toward the spectators. She seemed to look each individual in the eye; each bow seemed meant for that person alone. One seasoned diplomat noted that though the King looked "courteous, correct, and well-groomed like his pictures," he "lacked personality." The Queen, "verging on plumpness," highlighted the parade, and the multitude cheered and clapped lustily as she passed.

The motorcade drove into the south entrance of the White House, where, for the first time since the Civil War, soldiers stood guard with rifles and fixed bayonets. Inside the Executive Mansion foreign diplomats had gathered to receive the King and Queen. Because of rules of precedence China's ambassador stood with Japan's, and the representative of Franco's Spain paired off with his counterpart from the Soviet Union. After meeting with the diplomats the royal couple took a quick sightseeing drive around Washington. The tour ended prematurely so that the King and Queen might dress for the capital's main social event of the year, the garden party at the British Embassy.

On the embassy's extensive lawns, Washington society rubbed elbows, and then some, in a determined effort to stay near the royal presence and the punch bowls. Over a thousand uncomfortably dressed guests jammed the humid gardens. As one reporter remarked, going to the party was in itself an "excellent weight-reducing privilege." Having an invitation meant being "acceptable." Originally Lady Lindsay, the British ambassador's wife, had invited only a select group of congressmen and their wives, apparently following her husband's dictum that the garden party was like "heaven—some are taken and some are not." But when those omitted raised a storm of protest, the embassy expanded the guest list. Most congressmen finally received an invitation, and their wives dragged them to the embassy to mingle nonchalantly with

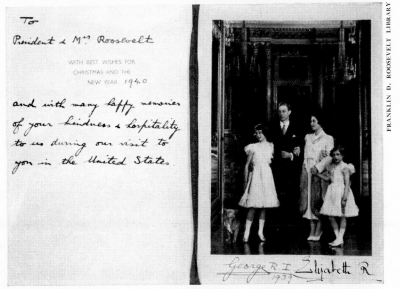

After Episcopal services Sunday morning, the Roosevelts and their guests posed outside St. James's Church, Hyde Park. Left to right: the Most Reverend Henry St. George Tucker, the Queen, the King, the President, his son James, his mother, his wife, and Prime Minister MacKenzie King of Canada. The royal train departed that night (far left). In December the Roosevelts received greetings (below) from their recent houseguests.

Mrs. Woodrow Wilson, J. P. Morgan, Jr., John D. Rockefeller, Jr., Mrs. Cornelius Vanderbilt, and Admiral Richard E. Byrd.

Secretary of the Interior Harold Ickes was invited but did not attend; he went instead to a stag cocktail party at the apartment of a young Texas congressman, Lyndon B. Johnson. Dressed in shirtsleeves, Ickes enjoyed Johnson's drinks, he later recalled, more than he would have "the formal doings in morning coat and silk hat at the British Embassy, milling about with a lot of uninteresting, climbing, and supercilious people." Most congressmen rejected Ickes' view of the affair and turned up at the embassy. Although Indiana's Sherman Minton and Rhode Island's Theodore F. Green drew criticism from their Senate colleagues for wearing full formal attire, others erred in the opposite direction. One senator defied convention by appearing in a lounge suit. Another sported a straw hat. Nevada's Pat McCarran thrust a green carnation in his lapel to remind the British of Irish-American Anglophobia. Arthur Vandenberg of Michigan appeared in an ice-cream suit, and a South Dakota senator wore a most proper cutaway but topped it with a Stetson.

Styles of dress were not the only compromises made with formality. The heat and humidity loosened the bindings of convention. Perspiring women fanned themselves with invitation-card envelopes and parched men struggled around the punch bowls for iced tea and lemonade, a scene which prompted Representative C. Jasper Bell to blurt out that the party "was sort of like our church socials in Missouri." King George tried to ease the situation by cracking "Finder's keepers!" when someone dropped a coin in the receiving line, but he did not stoop to pick it up himself. Vice President Garner succeeded in burying all protocol in the punch bowl when he dealt the King a Texas-style greeting—a hearty slap on the back. Ickes, when he heard of it, noted sarcastically in his diary that the slap was only "a showing of familiarity and bad breeding necessary to impress others with his democracy." Somehow able to ignore the congressional buffoonery, a diplomat concluded that the garden party, which had "caused more heartburns, more adverse press comment, [and] more of a tempest in a teapot than any social event . . . in this country, [went] off beautifully."

The formal state dinner that evening gave Garner another opportunity to display his "democracy." Sitting on the Queen's right, Cactus Jack was as "full of life as a kitten," Ickes noted. The Secretary of the Interior was shocked. Obviously, he told his diary, Garner had "no breeding or natural dignity," treating royalty as he would poker cronies. Ickes doubted "if

CONTINUED ON PAGE 108

This painting, Washington at Dorchester Heights, *is more than eight feet high; it was painted by Emanuel Leutze.*

Providence Rides a Storm

Had a tempest not thwarted his plans,
George Washington might have lost the Revolution
in the first major operation he commanded

By JAMES THOMAS FLEXNER

That George Washington drove the British out of Boston in early March, 1776, is known to almost every schoolboy who has studied the American Revolution, but a disturbing aspect of this crucial event is not recognized even by most of the experts. One may read biographies of Washington, and military histories of the Revolution, without coming on more than a stray hint. This omission has undoubtedly occurred because the story flies in the face of the traditional Washington legend. But a thorough study of the facts makes abundantly clear how innocent Washington was of military know-how in the early stages of the war, before he taught himself in the school of experience to be a soldier vastly superior to his professional opponents.

The maneuver that succeeded in driving the British out of Boston was only the first, and to Washington the less important, step in his strategic plan. The second half of the plan was aimed at nothing less than the annihilation of the British army. However, what Washington intended was so badly thought out and so foolhardy that it might well have resulted in the destruction of his own army. It is doubtful that in this early stage of the war, well before American independence had been declared, the patriot cause could have survived such a blow.

Everything was ready for the potentially disastrous effort when the unforeseeable intervened: the move was blocked by what lawyers call "an act of God"; Washington himself described it—ruefully, in disappointment—as "a remarkable interposition of Providence."

Ever since Washington had taken over the command of the Continental Army almost a year before, the war had been a stalemate. (The battles at Lexington and Concord and the one at Bunker Hill had been fought before Washington's arrival.) The British occupied two paddle-shaped peninsulas that stretched out into Boston Harbor: Boston Neck, on which the city of Boston stood, and Charlestown Neck, the broad end of which was separated from the city only by a minor channel. The narrow isthmuses where the two necks joined the mainland were so heavily fortified that no force could move across them in either direction, except under the most extraordinary circumstances. Along the jagged shore line of the intervening bay, Washington's army was encamped in defensive positions. He himself kept his headquarters in the university town of Cambridge, which was three miles back from the bay.

Such had been the situation when Washington joined his army. He had strengthened fortifications and drilled men and recruited and gathered supplies, but shortages of everything had plagued his efforts, and he had never been able to do anything toward advancing the cause. This was as anguishing to him as to anyone else. He had hoped to bring the matter to a conclusion and be back at his Virginia plantation by the fall of 1775, but winter arrived with nothing definite accomplished.

With the winter came snow, snow such as Washington had seldom encountered in Virginia. It imposed silence and seemed to dim out the world; yet as he lay sleepless in the dark, Washington felt "the Eyes of the whole Continent fixed with anxious expectation" upon him. He knew that he was being criticized for allowing a large and expensive army to sit motionless month after month. Although he did not put the whole blame on Congress for the chronic shortages he had suffered of money, arms, tents, gunpowder, and engineers—"I dare say the demands upon them are greater than they can supply"—he nonetheless found it discouraging that Congress seemed "to look upon this as the season for action, but will not furnish the means."

When morning came, he would go to the bay and jump up and down on the ice. There were times when he judged that it was strong enough to carry his army all the way to the British. Shortages or no, surely this presented an opportunity to be seized!

Accordingly, in mid-February, 1776, Washington notified a council of his general officers that their army had, or expected soon to have, 16,077 men. His spies reported that the enemy had only 5,000 fit for duty. These would be kept so busy by a "bold and resolute push" across the ice that the Americans would have to leave only a skeleton garrison to protect their camp and could bring virtually their whole force to bear, overwhelming the British. The battle might well "put a final end to the war and restore [the] peace and tranquillity so much wished for."

As he argued for such a battle, Washington scanned the faces of his generals without seeing any kindling of enthusiasm in their eyes. The reply came that with Tory irregulars the British numbered many more than 5,000 (this was correct); that 2,000 of the patriots lacked arms; that, in fact, a strong force would have to be left to hold the American lines. And, in any case, an assault should be preceded by several days of bombardment. Washington then asked whether the bombardment could be begun "with the present stock of powder." His officers voted to wait for an adequate supply, and the General concurred.

The decision to postpone everything, Washington commented to Congress, "being almost unanimous, I suppose must be right," yet he was still in favor of an immediate assault. Of course, "the irksomeness of my situation . . . might have inclined me to put more to the hazard than was consistent with prudence." Yet he had considered the matter very carefully. How the planter and wilderness fighter, long used to improvisation, emphasized will over means is revealed by his "firm hope" that, "if the men would have stood by me," an assault would have triumphed "notwithstanding the enemy's advantage of ground, artillery, etc."

For months, Washington had been developing an artillery corps of his own. Since he was perpetually urging his officers to make up for their lack of experience by reading, he was impressed by a very fat but surprisingly active young man who almost always had an artillery manual in his hand. On better acquaintance, Henry Knox proved to be strong (despite his obesity) as well as clever, gay, and amiable. Furthermore, whenever the former Boston bookseller had been given anything at all to work with, he had been able to improvise something that would function at least pretty well. The Massachusetts leaders also admired Knox. Washington had, therefore, put him in charge of the artillery. During the previous November, as soon as snow had smoothed rutty roads so that heavy objects could be pulled over them on sledges, Knox had been sent off to Ticonderoga, several hundred miles away, to fetch the cannon that had been captured with that royal fort. By early February, he had succeeded in dragging fifty-nine field pieces to Cambridge. Although many were rusty, cumbersome, and antiquated, the patriots felt that they now had, in Knox's words, "a noble train of artillery" (see "Big Guns for Washington" in the April, 1955, AMERICAN HERITAGE).

When his plan for attacking across the ice was abandoned, Washington worked out with his officers a plan for using this artillery. Penetrating the bay to the southeast of Boston Neck was still another peninsula, Dorchester. Inland on this broad neck, but still within two miles of Boston, were heights from which, so Washington wrote, cannon could "command a great part of the town and also the whole harbor." Furthermore, jutting out from the Dorchester peninsula on the Boston side was another hill, known as Nook's Hill, which was separated from the city only by a half-mile-wide channel. The council of general officers decided to prepare so that, when the necessary powder arrived, they could plant the cannon first on Dorchester Heights and then, if possible, on Nook's Hill.

The strategic importance of the hills had long been recognized by both commands. However, the Americans had been incapable of making effective use of them until Knox appeared with the cannon. And for the British to have occupied them would have overextended their lines, which were already long in relation to the size of their army. Furthermore, any British force on Dorchester would have been vulnerable to a surprise assault, since the peninsula abutted on the patriot-held mainland and was separated from Boston by water barely passable in bad weather.

Even after his spies had told him that Washington intended to fortify Dorchester Heights, General William Howe, the British commander, reasoned that he should let the rebels try and then, by blasting or driving them out before they could get a foothold, return the hills to their role as no man's land. He knew that the rebels were good at burying themselves like moles, but the ground was frozen too solid for such digging.

But for two months now Washington had been preparing materials that could be used for fortifications on frozen earth. Men not guarding the lines or building barracks had been kept busy tying together "fascines"—bundles of sticks about three feet thick and four feet long—or nailing up "chandeliers"—frames in which these fascines would be placed. Others had been collecting hay and twisting it into great bundles. Carts were now mobilized to carry all these supplies to Dorchester Heights, and spades were sharpened so that at least a little dirt could be hacked out of the frozen ground to hold the equipment down.

As these American preparations went on, the British seemed to be preparing to evacuate Boston. Four or five hundred men actually sailed away under the British second-in-command, General Henry Clinton. The rest of the shipping in the harbor was being mobilized, and some mortars were taken down from Bunker Hill.

Although Washington feared a feint to put him off his guard, there was the possibility that the British actually intended to move. A few months before, this prospect would have delighted him, as he would have assumed that the departing enemy was going back to England. But since then, public statements by George III had made it clear that the British would continue the war until they were defeated. Knowing that they had control of the ocean, Washington now had to assume that they would evacuate Boston only to move to some more strategically advantageous American harbor, probably New York. Since the patriots would then be in a worse position than now, more might be lost than gained by simply dislodging the British from Boston. Washington concluded that he should try to crush the British before they could get away.

British regulars, Washington reasoned, would not cravenly embark under the threat of guns placed on Dorchester. If the patriot positions could withstand the cannonading that would certainly be the enemy's first reaction—and Washington intended to see that they could—surely Howe would feel that the honor of his army required an assault with musket and bayonet. This would create another Bunker Hill, with the enemy forced, after crossing open water, to charge uphill against entrenched patriots firing down on them.

The ice having melted, Washington collected a flotilla of small boats in the Charles River, which flowed past Cambridge into the harbor. If the British should attack Dorchester Heights in sufficient numbers to weaken the Boston garrison, 4,000 patriots would climb into the little boats and cast off in two divisions.

After three "floating batteries" (each consisting of one twelve-pounder) had been rowed into position and had softened up the beachhead, the first wave would land on Boston Common and seize the two hills there, Beacon Hill and Mount Horam. The second wave would then land a little further south.

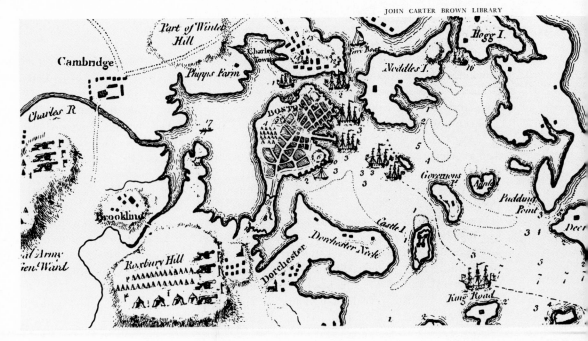

This detail of a British map, drawn in mid-1775 to illustrate the recent battles of Bunker Hill, Lexington, and Concord (called by the cartographer "the late Engagement between the King's Troops & the Provincials"), shows Boston Harbor with the three peninsulas, Dorchester, Boston, and Charlestown, jutting out from the mainland. Nook's Hill, not identified here, is on the finger of Dorchester Neck that points toward Boston, and Castle Island, just to the east of the neck, is the Castle William of this article.

The two forces would meet, advance against the unfortified rear of the British lines on Boston Neck, smash those lines, and let into town another patriot force that would be waiting at Roxbury. Then it would be just a matter of mopping up the British army.

Considering the plan "well digested," and made confident by "the cheerfulness and alacrity" of the subordinates to whom he had entrusted the preparations, Washington saw "reason to hope for a favorable and happy issue." Yet he was not entirely free of personal forebodings. To his wife's brother-in-law, Burwell Bassett, he expressed concern about his title to some wilderness lands at the confluence of the savage Kanawha and the wild Ohio: "In the worst event," they would serve him "for an asylum."

On February 27, Washington's general orders sent quakes of excitement and fear through the thousands of human beings around him: "As the season is now fast approaching when every man must expect to be drawn into the field of action, it is highly necessary that he should prepare his mind. . . ." The troops were bidden to remember that they were engaged in "the cause of virtue and mankind," and also that every man who skulked, hid, or retreated without orders would be *instantly shot down, as an example of cowardice.*"

Washington managed to secure a moderate stock of powder. He called in the local militia, whom he planned to have occupy his fortifications while the troops were out fighting. He recruited nurses and had two thousand bandages prepared. His council of officers had ruled that several days of preparatory bombardment should weaken the enemy and divert their attention from Dorchester, so the guns opened up on the city of Boston from the northern side of the line at about midnight on March 2. After many months of almost unbroken quiet, the sounds were shocking. Abigail Adams rushed to her door in nearby Braintree and ascertained that the firing was from "our army. . . . No sleep for me tonight!"

"From my window," wrote Lieutenant Samuel Webb of Connecticut, "[I] have a most pleasing and yet dismal view of the fiery ministers of death flying through the air. Poor inhabitants, our friends! We pity most sincerely, but particularly the women and children."

Washington counted the shots—only about twenty-five had been authorized because of the need to conserve powder—and was pleased to see that they carried well and seemed to be well aimed. However, there were several extraordinarily bright and loud flashes and bangs, which revealed that his inexperienced artillerymen had overloaded and burst their guns.

Eventually the British artillery answered. Their guns did not carry far enough to reach the American barracks. There was little call for the two thousand bandages.

The next night the patriots staged a similar bombardment, but the British responded more actively, making the roaring more formidable.

On the third night—it was March 4—the American batteries really opened up. Webb thought he heard from Boston "the cries of poor women and children." Washington was too busy for such hallucinations. As soon as darkness laid its sooty hands across British telescopes, movement throbbed through the American camp.

Regiments were paraded and only then were they told their specific missions (spies had to be frustrated). Safety, the officers pointed out, would depend on the enemy seeing no light and hearing no shout or accidental musket shot before the fortifications on Dorchester were completed.

Off the men went, under a fine moon. The riflemen, who led the advance across the neck, spread out along Dorchester's shore in the direction from which glowed the lights of Boston. They stared below those lights, scanning the little gray and silver waves lapping the shore for the possible black forms of enemy prows.

Now file after file of soldiers carried tools and muskets across the neck and up to the heights. Intermingled with them came hundreds of wagons: wagons loaded with fascines, with chandeliers, with tight bales of hay, with barrels filled with stones that could be rolled down the slopes onto invaders. After eager hands had unloaded them, the wagons turned; later they appeared again. More than a thousand men carried the portable ramparts into position; others scratched up with their sharpened spades a little earth to hold them down.

All was shadowy, but the moon, "shining" (as Washington wrote) "in its full luster," cast enough glimmer to enable the men to see what they were doing and to ascertain that the tall figure on a dark horse—riding everywhere, it seemed—was General Washington.

His nerves were tensed for any accidental burst of noise from Dorchester that might warn the enemy, but he heard only the creak of wheels, the soft clopping of horses' hoofs, the rustle of men, the thud of axes as fruit trees came down to make an abatis. The real noise came from the far side of the harbor, where American cannon were purposely fixing the attention of the British with their continuous roar. At one moment, Washington could have seen the awesome sight of seven shells in the air at once.

At three o'clock there began an eerie movement of silent bodies along the exposed causeway to and from the mainland. Three thousand tired, work-stained men marched toward their barracks through the half-mile-wide neck, while about three thousand fresh men came in to man the fortifications that had taken shape on the two highest hills and the tableland between.

The moon sank. The dark tightened. Then dawn infused a wan light into the clinging ground mist. The firing at the far end of the lines ceased. Finally, the fog lifted to reveal the half circle of bay. On Dorchester Heights there was the morning singing of birds. Away and below, Boston seemed quiet, since the patriots could not discern the newly awakened enemy officers staring back up toward them out of windows.

The British commanders had still been drinking toasts the night before when they received a report

British force wished to avoid a long wade through mudflats, they would have to take advantage of the high tide at noon. However, there was little bustle on the wharves. Instead, cannon were being wheeled out, pointed at Dorchester, elevated, and fired. The balls struck the hills below the forts. The gun crews then labored to get more height by burying the rear wheels. There were more reports, but the balls still did not reach high enough. After some hours the effort was abandoned; by this time it was too late to achieve anything on the noon tide. In the meantime, the patriots had been strengthening their fortifications on Dorchester Heights by planting six twelve-pounders and by bringing up field pieces.

Finally, increasing activity on the waterfront must

In this section of a panorama of the rebel-held mainland painted by a British officer in Boston, Dorchester Heights appears across the water, in the scene at left. At right center, on Boston's Beacon Hill, stands the large white house of John Hancock.

that the enemy was active on Dorchester Heights. However, the officers had gone to sleep content, certain that whatever the yokels were up to could easily be handled the next day. But when the mist rose, they saw revealed such a fortification as they had not believed possible. The engineering officer, Archibald Robertson, wrote that this was a "most astonishing night's work, and must have employed from 15 to 20,000 men," while a more poetic redcoat, identified only as "an officer of distinction," felt that the defenses surely had been "raised with an expedition equal to that of the Genii belonging to Aladdin's Wonderful Lamp."

The first step in Washington's plan had been sensationally successful. Now for the second and what he considered the more important step! Four thousand fresh men waited on the banks of the Charles to invade Boston, waited only for a major part of the British garrison to get into boats and sail away to assault Dorchester Heights.

Surely, Washington must have stared through his military glass from a convenient hill. What Boston streets he could distinguish were filled with gaping soldiers and civilians. He knew that if an attacking

have made Washington's heart leap with anticipation: troops—there seemed to be several thousands—were getting into small boats and were being rowed out, with field pieces, to transports. The transports sailed down to Castle William, a fortified island well situated to be the jumping-off place for an attack on Dorchester.

All was going according to Washington's plan. The next high tide, which would be at about midnight, would surely float the British to the peninsula. General John Thomas would keep his 3,000 Americans in their fortifications awaiting the advance up the hillsides, which could be expected at dawn. By then, the officers in charge of the American attacking force would have their men in the boats on the Charles, ready to move toward Boston as soon as the battle raged on Dorchester. The future of the continent seemed up for grabs.

But before the fateful night was due, the sky created its own unnatural night and there swooped down from overhead a majestic storm. "A wind more violent than anything I ever heard," was the verdict of a British soldier. "I never before felt such cold and distress," wrote an American rifleman, Daniel McCurtin. On

CONTINUED ON PAGE 98

TO MY VALENTINE

HOLIDAY POST CARDS

Besides its lasting art, every age has its kitsch, and because there is so much of it, this cheap popular art is pretty durable too. Consider this fine collection of holiday post cards, kindly lent to us by Mrs. Earl Moore of Weston, Connecticut. Cliché after cliché, these chromos march through the year's calendar of feast and folly, carefully missing the real point of every holiday—yet somehow, perhaps because sixty or seventy years have passed since they were mailed in their millions for a penny each, a certain charm has crept over them. There's George and his cherry tree, Abe, and (overleaf) a scoop of other fond figures. See that sneaky young man with the mistletoe? Wake up, Jane, wake up!

Leap Year

May I pop the ?

The Top o' the Mornin to you.

With Best Easter Wishes.

ince they kissed the lads they loved so dear, and sent them to the front.

Hallowe'en

4th of JULY

Thanksgiving Day

A MERRY CHRISTMAS

"a scandalous, malicious and

By THOMAS J. FLEMING

MAD TOM in A RAGE

"At a Court of general Sessions of the Peace, holden at Claverack, in and for the county of Columbia, it is presented that Harry Croswell, late of the city of Hudson, in the county of Columbia aforesaid, Printer, being a malicious and seditious man, and of a depraved mind and wicked and diabolical disposition, and also deceitfully, wickedly and maliciously devising, contriving and intending, Thomas Jefferson, Esquire, President of the United States of America, to detract from, scandalize, traduce, and vilify, and to represent him, the said Thomas Jefferson, as unworthy of the confidence, respect and attachment of the People of the said United States, . . . and wickedly and seditiously to disturb the Peace and tranquility as well of the People of the State of New York as of the United States; . . . the said Harry Croswell did on the ninth day of September, in the year of our Lord 1802, with force and arms, at the said city of Hudson, in the said county of Columbia, wickedly, maliciously and seditiously print and publish and cause and procure to be printed and published, a certain scandalous, malicious and seditious libel, in a certain paper or publication entitled 'The Wasp.' . . ."

All history is a mingling of the great and small, of kings losing kingdoms for want of a horseshoe nail, of presidents assassinated because a guard needed a smoke. But seldom has there been a stranger concatenation of the petty and the magnificent, the comic and the tragic, the trivial and the profound, than in the case of the *People v. Croswell*, in 1803. By an odd blend of good and bad luck, an obscure twenty-four-year-old printer wrote himself into the *Dictionary of American Biography*, established the libel law on which contemporary press freedom still rests, jarred the political security of President Thomas Jefferson, and indirectly helped to involve Alexander Hamilton in his fatal duel with Aaron Burr.

In 1803 the infant American Republic was running a high political fever. The ferocity of the verbal warfare raging between the Federalists, the party created

seditious libel"

Is it libel to say that the President of the United States tried to seduce his neighbor's wife—even if he did? Thomas Jefferson tried to gag the venomous editor of upstate New York's *Wasp;* Alexander Hamilton argued brilliantly in defense of journalistic candor

by Alexander Hamilton, and the Democratic-Republicans, led by President Jefferson, has rarely been matched in American politics, even by the diatribes of today's New Left and Ultra Right.

The first fusillades had been fired during Washington's Presidency. The Jeffersonians, with not a little help from the Sage of Monticello himself, had set up journalists such as Philip Freneau and Benjamin Franklin Bache with one mission, to deflate and discredit an administration that was, in Jefferson's view, "galloping fast into monarchy." They soon had the Father of His Country in a state of near apoplexy. "That rascal Freneau," as Washington called him, insisted on sending his scurrilous *National Gazette,* published in Philadelphia, to the President's house even after he had cancelled his subscription. Freneau spent most of his abuse on Hamilton. Bache preferred Washington as a target, calling him "treacherous," "mischievous," "inefficient," and sneering at his "farce of disinterestedness" and his "stately journeyings through the American continent in search of personal incense."

These verbal guerrillas soon had imitators. Among the more savage was William Duane, Bache's successor as editor of the Philadelphia *Aurora.* Washington, he wrote, had "discharged the loathings of a sick mind." Even this was topped by an English newcomer, James T. Callender. In the Richmond *Examiner* he declared that "Mr. Washington has been twice a traitor."

The Federalists, the upholders of upper-class dignity, labored under a difficult handicap in such a war. They soon became afraid, in Washington's words, that "there seems to be no bounds to . . . attempts to destroy all confidence, that the People might, and . . . ought to have, in their government; thereby dissolving it, and producing a disunion of the States." The Alien and Sedition Acts of 1798 were an expression of this fear. Passed by a Federalist Congress with Washington's public approval, the Alien Act gave President John Adams the power to deport any foreigners he deemed

While less gentlemanly journalistic collaborators bludgeoned away at Thomas Jefferson in cartoons like the one opposite, Alexander Hamilton thrust a deft oratorical rapier at the Democratic-Republicans in the Croswell libel trial.

Harry Croswell—portrayed here as an Anglican priest a good many years after his trial for seditious libel—would have remained an obscure upstate New York citizen except for two things. As the young editor of the Wasp, *he had a wicked way with words; and he was attacking the Jeffersonians in the home county of New York's Jeffersonian attorney general, Ambrose Spencer. That was looking for trouble, and Croswell soon was in it right up to his stinger.*

dangerous to public peace. The Sedition Act empowered the federal judiciary to punish anyone convicted of false or malicious writing against the nation, the President, or Congress with a fine of not more than $2,000 and imprisonment for not more than two years.

Federalist judges immediately went to work and soon had indictments against Bache, Duane, Callender, and a dozen other Democratic-Republican editors. The Jeffersonians responded at the state level with the Kentucky and Virginia resolutions of 1798, which declared the Alien and Sedition Acts altogether void and introduced the doctrine of nullification into American constitutional thinking—a seed that would bear ominous fruit in a later era. Up and down the land, Jeffersonian editors bellowed mightily that the Federalists were attempting to erase the First Amendment and destroy the free press.

The Jeffersonian counterattack was beautifully executed: the Federalist judges retreated in disarray and all but abandoned the unpopular prosecutions after a mere ten convictions. The nation roared into the election of 1800 with both sides strenuously exercising their right of free speech. But except for a few slugging editors who sneered at "Massa Jefferson" the slave owner, most of the Federalist propaganda came from pulpits, where clergymen pictured the election of the pro-French and "atheistic" Jefferson as the beginning of a Jacobinical reign of terror against religion. In the print shops the Jeffersonians had the bigger, more vituperative guns. James Callender's pamphlet, *The Prospect Before Us,* slandered Washington and Adams with such recklessness that it achieved an unenviable literary fame. Although Federalist papers theoretically outnumbered the Jeffersonians 103 to 64, most of them maintained a tepid semineutrality that permitted the Democratic-Republicans to run away with public opinion and the election. Defeated John Adams wrote mournfully, "If we had been blessed

A much more prominent candidate for a libel suit on the part of the Jeffersonians against scurrilous Federalist editors was William Coleman, of the New York Evening Post. *A protégé of Hamilton's who translated his mentor's political views into inflammatory but scintillating satire on the Democratic-Republicans, he was widely read and quoted. But Hamilton was sure to leap to his aid; so the Jeffersonians picked on Croswell. Then Hamilton came to his aid.*

with common sense, we should not have been overthrown by Philip Freneau, Duane, Callender. . . . A group of foreign liars have discomfited the education, the talents, the virtues, and the property of the country."

But the Federalists were down, not out. Older leaders like John Jay might retire to their estates in dismay, but there were numerous young, vigorous Federalists in the prime of middle life, such as Hamilton and Fisher Ames of Massachusetts, who did not feel it was time for them to abandon politics. They decided Federalism was not dead, it had just been misrepresented, distorted, and smeared without rebuttal. It was time to junk the older Federalist ideas about the vulgarity of appealing to the people through the press. Ames suggested a Latin motto as a guide: *Fas est et ab hoste doceri* ("It is perfectly proper to be taught by one's enemy"). Up and down the Republic, Federalists began founding papers in which, Ames

declared, "wit and satire should flash like the electrical fire." At the same time, the paper he helped found, the *New England Palladium*, would, he predicted, be "fastidiously polite and well-bred. It should whip Jacobins as a gentleman would a chimney sweeper, at arms length, and keeping aloof from his soot."

In New York, Alexander Hamilton soon gathered a group of well-heeled Federalists who put up $10,000 for a daily to be called the *Evening Post* (still in business today, as the *New York Post*). Its editor, William Coleman, met Alexander Hamilton by night and took down his editorials from the very lips of the great man himself. Throughout the other states, similar papers suddenly blossomed: in Baltimore, for example, the *Republican, or, Anti-Democrat;* in South Carolina, the Charleston *Courier.* In Hudson, New York, another group of Federalists led by Elisha Williams, one of the state's most noted attorneys, backed Ezra Sampson as the editor of the *Balance and Columbian Re-*

pository. As a junior editor Sampson hired twenty-two-year-old Harry Croswell.

Connecticut born, this well-built, dignified young man had studied for a time in the household of Noah Webster, later of dictionary fame and a high Federalist of the old school. (Webster's solution for rampant Jeffersonianism was to raise the voting age to forty-five.) Temperamentally, Harry Croswell was a born Federalist. He was religious, had a natural deference for older, wiser, richer men, and tended to see political developments of the day as a clash between the forces of darkness and light.

Hudson at this time was not the somnolent little river town it is today. In the decade after the Revolution it carried more ships on its registers than the city of New York. Much of western Massachusetts and northern Connecticut used Hudson for a shipping center. One March day in 1802, a reporter counted 2,800 sleighs loaded with goods on Hudson's streets, creating a traffic jam of prodigious dimensions. At the

THE WASP.

By Robert Rusticoat, Esquire.

Vol. I.]   " *To lash the Rascals naked through the world.*"   [No. 6.

HOLT says, the burden of the Federal song is, that Mr. Jefferson paid Callender for writing against the late administration.   This is wholly false.   The charge is explicitly this :—Jefferson paid Callender for calling Washington a traitor, a robber, and a perjurer—For calling Adams, a hoary headed incendiary ; and for most grossly slandering the private characters of men, who, he well knew were virtuous.   These charges, not a democratic editor has yet dared, or ever will dare to meet in an open manly discussion.

Rhetorically quite mild, this passage still libelled Jefferson so "explicitly" as to count heavily against Croswell.

same time, with Albany, the state capital, a mere twenty-eight miles upriver, it was hardly surprising that Hudson and surrounding Columbia County were politically sensitive areas. Later in the century one local historian unabashedly claimed that the county had produced more distinguished politicians than any other comparable area in the entire country.

The Jeffersonians were strongly entrenched there. In 1802, the attorney general of the state of New York was sharp-eyed, hatchet-faced Ambrose Spencer, a native son of Columbia County. Morgan Lewis, chief justice of the state supreme court, was married to Gertrude Livingston, whose family's vast upstate hold-

ings included a large chunk of the southern portion of the county. The Livingstons were the most potent voice in the Jeffersonian party at that time.

It was hardly surprising, therefore, that the Jeffersonians decided to set up a rival to the Federalist *Balance*. For their printer they chose Charles Holt, former editor of the New London *Bee* and a Sedition Act martyr who had been convicted in 1800 for libel and spent several months in jail. Holt prepared to launch a *Bee* in Hudson and made it clear it would buzz impertinently in the face of the dignified *Balance*.

Young Harry Croswell forthwith saw an opportunity to prove his extreme devotion to Federalism. He persuaded his senior editor, Sampson, to let him publish in the garret of the *Balance* office a paper entitled the *Wasp*. As an editorial pseudonym, Croswell chose "Robert Rusticoat"; for a motto, "To lash the Rascals naked through the world." Down in New York, an observer in the *Evening Post* told the story in doggerel obviously modelled on "Yankee Doodle."

> *There's Charlie Holt is come to town*
> *A proper lad with types, sir.*
> *The Democrats have fetched him here*
> *To give the federals stripes, sir.*
>
> *The Balance-folks seem cruel 'fraid*
> *That he'll pull down their scales, sir.*
> *And so they got a pokerish wasp,*
> *To sting him with his tail, sir.*

Croswell's opening number was nothing less than a declaration of war:

Wherever the Bee ranges, the Wasp will follow over the same fields and on the same flowers—Without attempting to please his friends, the Wasp will only strive to displease, vex and torment his enemies ... The Wasp has a dirty and disagreeable job to perform. He has undertaken the chastisement of a set of fellows who are entrenched in filth—who like lazy swine are wallowing in a puddle. He must therefore wade knee deep in smut before he can meet his enemies on their own ground.

At his opposite number, Holt, Croswell levelled the following blast:

It is well known that you was bro't here by virtue of $500 raised for that purpose by the leading Democrats in this city. That the public may know, therefore, with how much purity and independence you will conduct in your editorial labors, would you be kind enough to answer the following questions:

Did the contributors to the $500 purchase you, as they purchase Negroes in Virginia, or hire you as they hire servants in New England?

Are you not a mere automaton in the hands of your masters; pledged to publish whatever slanders or falsehoods they shall dictate? And by your contract with them if you refuse to pollute your sheets have they not a right to ship you back again to your 350 subscribers in New London?

Croswell soon made it clear that this was more than a local war. Down in Virginia, James Callender was demonstrating his lack of principle by turning on his former idol, Thomas Jefferson. After Jefferson became President, Callender, working on the assumption that his slanderous attack on Washington and Adams had done much to swing the election, coolly asked to be made postmaster of Richmond. Jefferson declined, whereupon Callender revealed in print that while he was working on *The Prospect Before Us*, Jefferson had sent him a hundred dollars and had even read part of the manuscript, returning it with the declaration, "Such papers cannot fail to produce the best affect. They inform the thinking part of the nation..."

This was sensational stuff, the kind of thing that could hurt Jefferson politically. Washington was now in his grave two years and already the process of canonization was in full swing. Federalist printers rushed to their presses to discuss Jefferson's rather lame explanation that he had sent Callender the hundred dollars out of charity, and because he was a Sedition Act victim. But few equalled the savagery with which the *Wasp* pilloried this explanation.

It amounts to this then. He [Jefferson] read the book and from that book inferred that Callender was an object of charity. Why! One who presented a face bloated with vices, a heart black as hell—one who could be guilty of such foul falsehoods, such vile aspersions of the best and greatest man the world has yet known—he an object of charity! No! He is the very man, that an aspiring mean and hollow hypocrite would press into the service of crime. He is precisely qualified to become a tool—to spit the venom and scatter the malicious, poisonous slanders of his employer. He, in short, is the very man that a dissembling patriot, pretended "man of the people" would employ to plunge for him the dagger, or administer the arsenic.

Again and again Croswell sank his stinger into this Jeffersonian blister.

Will the reader turn to that inaugural speech of 1801 and see how this incarnate [Jefferson] speaks of Washington. There he makes him a demigod—having already paid Callender for making him a devil...Will the word hypocrite describe this man? There is not strength enough in the term.

When Holt attempted to answer Croswell by impugning Callender's character, the young Federalist editor hoisted him with another petard.

About the time of Callender's trial, you [Holt] printed a paper in New London—in that paper Callender was extolled to the skies. He was then an "excellent Republican," a "virtuous man," a "good citizen," a "suffering patriot."...If there is anything on earth to be pitied, it is a miser-"able editor" constantly tumbling into the mire; and whose every struggle but sinks him deeper.

The disarray of his antagonists emboldened Croswell to aim some shafts at local Democratic-Republicans. In the September 9, 1802, issue of the *Wasp* appeared the following poem:

> Th' attorney general chanc'd one day to meet
> A dirty, ragged fellow in the street
>   A noisy swaggering beast
>   With rum half drunk at least
> Th' attorney, too, was drunk—but not with grog—
> Power and pride had set his head agog.

The poem went on to describe how the attorney general, "madly frowning on the clown," asked him how he had the insolence to address him as a "fellow lab'rer for the common good."

> "Why," said the fellow with a smile,
> "You weekly in the paper toil,
> "Condemn the old administration
> "And do your best to 'save the nation'
> "While I with just the same pretenses
> "Chalk 'Damn the Feds' on gates and fences."

Croswell lampooned other leading local characters who were perfectly recognizable even when he named no names. One satire described a prominent judge who spent an evening eating and drinking at a nearby tavern and then refused to pay his bill. In a memoir that he attached to one of the few surviving complete sets of the *Wasp* (now at the New-York Historical Society), Croswell told how he was walking through the streets of Hudson, not long after publication of the latter tale, when up thundered a local justice of the peace, a big man named Hagedorn, who leaped off his wagon, shook his horsewhip under Croswell's nose, and vowed that he considered the tavern story slander and was going to extract instant revenge.

"I had no cane or other means of defense," Croswell wrote. "But I stood erect and dropping my hands to my sides looked him full in the face and in the most cool and collected manner apprised him that... neither he nor any other man could ever whip me and it was a mistake for him to talk so loud about it. He...broke out again in a tempest of oaths, turned shortly on his heel, mounted his wagon and drove off at a furious pace, his poor horse having received the rash intended for me."

Looking around him, Croswell noticed a staunch Federalist friend in a nearby doorway laughing heartily at the exchange. "Harry Croswell," said he, "how

CONTINUED ON PAGE 100

27

On an unseasonably warm evening in April, 1866, a well-tailored gentleman with a drooping mustache and a long, thin face, obviously a member of the "upper ten," stood at the intersection of Fifth Avenue and Twenty-third Street in New York City, watching the tangle of traffic where Broadway slants across Fifth Avenue. A wilder individualism than we know today prevailed among the horsecars and omnibuses, the struggling carriages, drays, vans, and butchers' carts of New York. Every wheel was turned, of course, by horsepower. Suddenly the observer stepped off the curb and threaded his way toward a teamster who was giving his weary workhorse an unmerciful beating.

"My friend," he said, "you can't do that any more."

"Can't beat my own horse," the teamster shot back, "—the devil I can't," as he fell to again.

"You are not aware, probably, that you are breaking the law," said the interloper, "but you are. I have the new statute in my pocket; and the horse is yours only to treat kindly. I could have you arrested. I only want to inform you what a risk you run."

"Go to hell," snapped the teamster, amazed. "You're mad!"

Thus Henry Bergh began, quietly and politely, but firmly, a twenty-two-year effort to arouse the American conscience to the plight of fellow creatures who could not defend themselves or explain their predicament. Earlier that day, the nineteenth of April, the New York state legislature had passed a bill punishing an act, or omission of an act, that caused pain to animals "unjustifiably." It was a historic step forward in the nineteenth-century movement toward animal protection.

It became one of Bergh's most effective arguments to stress the *cost* of cruelty to the more than eighty-five million animals "contributing in one way or another to the daily support and enrichment of the people of this country." Cruel treatment of cows resulted in contaminated butter, cheese, and milk. The horrors of the cattle train endangered the meat supply. The aphorism "horses are cheaper than oats" lost its specious appeal when in 1872 two thirds of all the horses in New York City were stricken with a deadly respiratory disease, producing, said Bergh, "a panic among the human inhabitants"; thousands walked, and the flow of urban life slowed to a trickle.

For twenty-two years Henry Bergh—who faintly resembled a number of his canine friends—was the controversial man behind the president's badge of the society he had created.

In Henry Bergh—a reformed dilettante who founded the A.S.P.C.A.— many saw a latter-day Saint Francis of Assisi. But others, especially the cruel or the thoughtless, regarded him as

THE GREAT MEDDLER

By GERALD CARSON

Cruelty to animals was not an offense under common law unless it carried with it a public nuisance factor, *i.e.,* was observable and offensive to humans or violated a property right. There were animal-protection statutes in certain states, including New York, but they were narrowly drawn, usually for the purpose of protecting some property interest. Machinery for enforcement was lacking; the laws were largely ineffective.

Just a few days before the New York legislature passed the animal-welfare act of 1866, it had chartered an animal-protection society. The new organization, the first of its kind in the Western Hemisphere, was called the American Society for the Prevention of Cruelty to Animals. The A.S.P.C.A.'s sponsors were prominent New Yorkers, leaders in the city, state, and nation in finance, commerce, the law, and politics. But the driving force behind the anticruelty idea was Henry Bergh. He was the founder, president, inspirer, advocate, diplomatist, lecturer, writer, administrator, fund raiser, and tireless protestant against the abuse of animals and against indifference to man's effect upon their condition and environment.

"To plant, or revive, the principle of mercy in the human heart," Bergh said, would be "a triumph . . . greater than the building of the Great Pacific Railroad."

The cause became known as "Bergh's War." The A.S.P.C.A. was the "Bergh Society," its agents were "Bergh's men." Henry Bergh's tall, muscular figure and long, sad-eyed face—as he patrolled the streets, appeared in courtrooms, or stopped in at the American Museum to see how Barnum was treating his menagerie—became as familiar to New Yorkers as William Cullen Bryant's magnificent white beard or Horace Greeley's long white duster and old white hat.

There was little in Henry Bergh's heritage or earlier life to suggest his remarkable ability to see the human world through the eyes of a wounded bird, a cat stuck in a drain pipe, the animals pacing their cages in the Central Park Zoo, or the biblical Balaam's ass, which, when the Lord opened her mouth, reproached her master: "What have I done unto thee, that thou hast smitten me these three times?"

The descendant of a notable family that had emigrated in the eighteenth century from the Rhenish Palatinate to the mid-Hudson Valley, Henry Bergh was the youngest of three children of Christian Bergh, a stern Jacksonian Democrat and prosperous shipbuilder in New York City during the first forty years of the century. Henry was born on August 29, probably in 1813, in a two-story frame house at the northeast corner of Scammel and Water streets.* It stood within the sound of the axes, adzes, saws, and hammers at the family shipyard at Corlear's Hook, where Manhattan shouldered out into the East River toward Williamsburg and the Navy Yard.

Bergh entered Columbia College in 1830 with some thought of a career in law. As a collegian he was a young man of fashion, enjoying the balls and the company of the town wits. Preferring the pleasures of travel to the life of study, he dropped out of Columbia and, after tasting Europe, turned his thoughts to marriage. In 1839, he wedded Catherine Matilda Taylor, daughter of an English architect practicing in New York. With Christian Bergh's death in 1843, the shipyard was closed, and Henry and his wife, childless and well off (contemporaries put their wealth at several hundred thousand to a million dollars), travelled and lived extensively in Europe. They also built an elaborate residence on Fifth Avenue and, when stateside, moved in the social circles of Saratoga and Washington, as well as New York.

In Europe, Bergh reacted rapturously to the right things—the Parthenon, the Tirol, the cathedral at Cologne. Nor did he neglect the pleasures of the palate: he savored the great white wines of the Rhine Valley and the fine pâté of Strasbourg. A hint of the future came in Seville, where the Berghs attended a bullfight and were revolted as some eight bulls were killed and twenty horses eviscerated.

Sometimes Bergh carried official dispatches, which entitled him to a "cabinet passport" and immunity from prying customs officers. The couple was in favor at various American legations, and attended soirées at the Elysée during the presidency of Louis Napoleon. The American minister at the Court of St. James's, Abbott Lawrence, presented Bergh to Prince Albert, and later he was escorted to the House of Commons, where he saw Sir Robert Peel and Lord John Russell. In 1850, he visited Russia and was shown through the Kremlin. He liked the country, especially the nobility and the people's attitude toward Americans. "There are many points of resemblance between Russia and the United States," he wrote, noting in particular two of the less flattering—slavery and widespread corruption in high places.

Bergh turned to literature and diplomacy, since the American government was dispatching a number of literary envoys—this was the era of Washington Irving in Madrid, George Bancroft in Berlin, Bayard Taylor in St. Petersburg, and John Bigelow in Paris. Moreover, Bergh was critical of many American diplomats he had met, considering them less accustomed than

* There is some confusion about the date of Bergh's birth, to which he himself contributed by treating the event, in his later years, as a movable feast.

himself to the ceremonious side of diplomatic life.

As an author Bergh was, unhappily, a poet *manqué* and an unsuccessful though persistent playwright (he often attempted humor, a trait in which he was extraordinarily deficient). He was, briefly, more fortunate in diplomacy. Early in 1863, President Lincoln named him to succeed Taylor as legation secretary at the court of Czar Alexander II, and there he served under the colorful southern abolitionist, Cassius Marcellus Clay (see "The Roar of the Aged Lion" in the June, 1960, AMERICAN HERITAGE). Bergh dreamed of a ministerial position in Europe, but disillusionment was quick in coming.

"Because of Clay's apprehensions that one of his underlings would become more popular with the Russians than he," wrote his most recent biographer, Professor David L. Smiley, ". . . he mistreated them all. Clay's jealousy erupted, and Bergh soon returned to the United States." He did so reluctantly, lingering in London for five months while he maneuvered for a new appointment. He appealed to a number of men in power at home, and finally to Lincoln himself—all to no avail.

But his one diplomatic assignment had left Bergh a lasting legacy. While in Russia, he had watched the peasants beat their horses and had, from the legation carriage, directed his splendidly liveried Vladimir or Alexander to order the droshky drivers to stop it. "At last," he commented, "I've found a way to utilize my gold lace." This was the turning point in Bergh's life toward his true mission.

Yet he admitted that he had never been particularly interested in animals. Once when he was calling on Miss Clara Morris, a leading emotional actress of the period, he drew back when her small dog put a friendly, inquiring paw on his knee. And he had even been capable of actions which, in his later years, he would have been the first to condemn. An entry in an early Bergh diary tells of an evening in Athens when, "as every other amusement had been exhausted, we gentlemen sallied out and stoned the dogs with which the city abounds."

Not as one devoted to pets, then, nor again out of a sentimental flinching at happenings that caused animals pain, but rather because of a kind of abstract concept of justice, Bergh seems to have undertaken his lifework as spokesman for those who could not speak for themselves. Yet one wonders if that quite covers it. Horses, one feels, must have been his secret passion. His speeches, lectures, and reports were filled with affectionate praise of "that generous and faithful servant, the horse" and "that noble creature, the horse." Why else did this reserved New Yorker, who looked like a blend of Quaker and French count,

The abuse of animals against which Bergh campaigned permeated all levels of society. New York's riffraff, often seeming to take on some of the characteristics of the contestants themselves, patronized dog pits like the one above. The everyday street scene included tradesmen beating their horses, below, and in fashionable parlors ladies smoked cigarettes while their dogs entertained them in rat baiting.

wear a gold horse's-head scarfpin in the folds of his black satin cravat and recall, in one of those classical allusions of which he was so fond, how Darius owed his crown to the neighing of a horse? "What struck me most forcibly," Bergh declared, "was that mankind derived immense benefits from these creatures, and gave them in return not the least protection."

Before leaving London for New York in June of 1865, Bergh was introduced to the Earl of Harrowby, president of the Royal Society for the Prevention of Cruelty to Animals, then in its forty-first year. Stimulated by what he learned of the service rendered by the R.S.P.C.A., Bergh decided to found a similar society in the United States, modelled upon the English pattern. The advancement of "merciful principles," he assured Lord Harrowby, was the "long cherished dream of my heart."

After careful preparatory work, Bergh unveiled his proposal on the stormy night of February 8, 1866, at New York's Clinton Hall. He had assembled a small but impressive audience which included the mayor (later the governor of New York), John T. Hoffman, and the department-store king A. T. Stewart. Frederick A. Conkling, soldier and merchant, occupied the chair while Henry Bergh spoke.

"Last evening," read the *New York Times*'s one-sentence report, "Henry Bergh, Esq., delivered a lecture on 'Statistics Relating to the Cruelties Practised upon Animals,' before the members of the American Geographical and Statistical Society, with a view to the establishment of a society kindred to that so long in successful operation in London, and in the other cities of Great Britain and Ireland."

Noting in a quick historical survey what had happened to animals (and humans too) in the Roman arena, the tortures inflicted in the Spanish bullring, and the brutalities of modern French vivisectionists, Bergh denounced the blood sports popular in New York, the abuse of horses by street railway and omnibus companies, and the barbarities that accompanied the transportation and slaughter of food animals.

"This is a matter purely of conscience," he concluded. "It has no perplexing side issues. . . . it is a moral question in all its aspects. . . . It is a solemn recognition of that greatest attribute of the Almighty Ruler of the Universe, mercy, which if suspended in our case but for a single instant, would overwhelm and destroy us."

Support came at once from Mayor Hoffman and Stewart, from Peter Cooper, manufacturer, inventor, philanthropist; from John Jacob Astor, II; Henry Clews, the banker; James Lenox, inventor and book collector; John A. Dix, soldier, cabinet officer, and future governor of New York; the publishing Harper brothers, and two Roosevelts—C. V. S., a wealthy merchant, and his brother, James J., attorney and jurist. Hamilton Fish, Bryant, and Greeley also endorsed a paper Bergh circulated outlining the objectives of the proposed society, and James T. Brady, leading New York attorney, drew up its charter. Ezra Cornell had a hand in the passage of the law that made it a misdemeanor to abuse "any horse, mule, cow, cattle, sheep or *other animal*" (italics supplied). Bergh was elected president of the A.S.P.C.A., and other prestigious names were added as officers, board members, and financial supporters. Bergh forwarded the names of his colleagues to the Earl of Harrowby, commenting with satisfaction that "the social and political rank of these gentlemen in their own country, correspond with that of the distinguished men who grace the record of the Parent Institution."

Bergh now had at his disposal an effective law and a private society clothed with public authority. Bergh himself was empowered by the attorney general of the state and the district attorney for the city to represent them in all cases involving the law for the protection of animals. In later years, as conditions improved, educational activities and relief work for disabled, sick, injured, or unwanted animals became more important than arresting and punishing offenders. This gain was due in part to the same influences that led to the emancipation of the slaves, prison reform, the temperance and woman's-rights movements, minimum-wage laws, the organization of the Red Cross, protection of women and children against economic exploitation, and concern over the plight of the insane. Another circumstance helped: the A.S.P.C.A. was able to secure convictions in over ninety per cent of all cases that reached the courts.

Bergh hoped that the word "American" in the title of the society would come to stand for a national organization. But the charter, under New York laws, was not appropriate elsewhere, and the idea of branches outside New York state proved impractical. The A.S.P.C.A.'s influence, however, was national, for many state and municipal societies quickly came into being; those in Massachusetts, Pennsylvania, New Jersey, and San Francisco were among the earliest. They adopted the A.S.P.C.A. seal (behind a teamster flailing a fallen horse stands an angel with a drawn sword and an upraised hand) and applied the humanitarian experience gained in New York. Within five years, an astonishingly short time for the penetration of a new idea, nineteen states and the Dominion of Canada had established societies of similar character.

From a little upstairs room at Broadway and

Fourth Street, plainly furnished with a Manila carpet and a few chairs, Bergh reached out to enlist support —to former President Millard Fillmore in Buffalo, urging him to establish a branch there; to Mrs. William Appleton in Boston and her associate in reform, George T. Angell; to Mrs. Caroline Earle White in Philadelphia. "Keep continually before the public," he counselled Angell. "Let us strive to excel one another." The president of the A.S.P.C.A. thought his task in New York the hardest. New York, he said, was in effect a foreign city, "composed of the refuse of European barbarism."

There was a coarseness in New York life a hundred years ago that gave the A.S.P.C.A. no small range of activity. Wealthy sportsmen held pigeon shoots in which live birds were first damaged in a wing or blinded in one eye, to create interesting flight patterns. At the other end of the social scale, the low-life sporting fraternity flocked to the dog and rat pits. At Kit Burns's Sportsmen's Hall at 273 Water Street, bulldogs fought black bears in the tradition of medieval bearbaiting. Terriers, competing against time, killed a hundred brown wharf rats in a zinc-lined enclosure, and as a special finale, Kit's son-in-law, Reddy the Blacksmith, would for the price of a glass of beer bite a live rat in two.

Henry Bergh seemed to be everywhere, fearlessly raiding the dog and rat pits and cocking mains, and working boldly in the streets. He made his first arrest when he sighted a butcher named Mans transporting live calves roped tightly together and stacked up like cordwood (sometimes the animals' heads hung out over the sides of transport carts and were crushed against passing vehicles or were ground against the wheels of their own cart). Bergh chased the cart all the way from Broadway to the Williamsburg Ferry and got a conviction. The president of the A.S.P.C.A. carried a cane that could be used as a weapon of defense, but usually a lifted finger and a glimpse of his official badge were sufficient to stop the carter with an overloaded dray or the butcher caught plucking live poultry. In addition to nabbing offenders, Bergh spent long hours in the Court of Special Sessions, where he was formidable in cross-examination, or atop the bleak hill at the Capitol in Albany, appearing before legislative committees. Meanwhile, he carried on the routine business of the society, cajoling the editors of New York's fifteen daily newspapers, writing tracts on vivisection and the care of the horse, lecturing, and raising money. "My time by day and night," he wrote to a correspondent, "is devoted to the Institution which I have founded."

Yet his life was not without its rewards. Bergh was an authoritarian at heart. Some of his contempo-

CULVER PICTURES

Bergh to the rescue: *Above, he helps an overworked friend; below, he and his men give an object lesson to a footman, stripping off his coat on a frigid day to demonstrate the suffering of milady's unblanketed horses. At bottom, Bergh accosts a driver whose team is smarting under the influences of a whip and burr bits. (The scene is Madison Square, where the arm of the partially completed Statue of Liberty had been set up to encourage donations for the pedestal.)*

BETTMANN ARCHIVE

CULVER PICTURES

raries would have chosen the harsher word "despot." But there was no doubt that the A.S.P.C.A. was Bergh and Bergh was the A.S.P.C.A. He clearly enjoyed the exercise of his considerable power, and had in his temperament that certain element of fanaticism necessary to the success of a great reform movement. Said one newspaper editor, saluting Bergh, "He who doeth one thing is terrible!"

One blustery winter night at the rush hour, with slush ankle-deep in the streets, Bergh concentrated his forces at Chatham Street (now Park Row), where a half dozen car lines converged. Bergh and his men ordered every horse that was lame or sick out of the traces. The condition of the wretched street-railway horses was notorious: it was not uncommon then to find parts of the harness embedded in an animal's flesh. That night there was plenty of work for the A.S.P.C.A. men. The result was a virtual blockade. Thousands of New Yorkers had to foot it uptown, growling, cursing, hungry, wet, and fighting mad. "Who did this?" was asked on all sides. And the answer came, "Bergh."

In the face of such criticism, Bergh was always urbane. But there was a hint of menace in his letters to indolent or uninterested judges, to newspaper editors careless of their facts, or, as an instance, to Tiffany & Company, whose wagon, he pointed out, the night before at about seven o'clock, on Fifth Avenue below Twenty-third Street, was drawn by a horse unfit for service. Bergh was precise. When he wrote to the police captain in West Thirty-fifth Street about a horse that had been abandoned in the gutter to die, he gave the name of the owner, the name and address of the man who committed the act, and the name and address of a witness. When Bergh complained to William H. Vanderbilt about a "dead lame" horse owned by the New York and Harlem Railroad, he gave the date and identified the horse as being attached to Fourth Avenue car No. 30. "I have adopted a habit through life," he wrote to a justice who was delaying unreasonably on a horse-abandonment case, "of always pursuing a subject until it is brought to its legitimate conclusion."

Applying to his animal-welfare objectives P. T. Barnum's operating philosophy about publicity—"I don't care much what the papers say about me, provided they will say something"—Henry Bergh undertook to overcome apathy through developing a spectacular case: the amelioration of torments visited upon green turtles. The turtles, the source of soup and succulent steaks, were transported by sailing ships from the tropics to the Fulton Fish Market in New York; they lay on their backs for several weeks, without food or water, held in place by ropes strung through holes punched in their flippers. Bergh boarded a schooner engaged in the turtle trade, arrested the captain and crew, and marched them off to The Tombs. He reinforced his position with a letter from Professor Louis Agassiz, the famous Harvard zoologist, assuring him that turtles could feel hunger, thirst, and pain and had, besides, certain minimal rights. A skeptical judge acquitted the defendants by holding that a turtle was not an animal within the meaning of the law. The case was a nine-day wonder, with the newspapers making extensive facetious comments on the nature of turtles and aggressive humanitarians.

"The day following," Bergh told a lecture audience, "the *Herald* devoted six columns to an account of the trial . . . and to the funny fellow who wrote that account I have always felt grateful, for his ridicule awakened the public from its apathy. Next day one million people understood my purpose and in a week, twenty millions knew there was a society for the defense of inferior animals."

Bergh tried on several subsequent occasions to come to the rescue of Florida turtles. It was one of his few failures. Even his best friends were embarrassed. Americans were not ready to extend their concern about animal welfare to a cold-blooded species. Nor, though they could get excited about cruelties practiced upon such domestic friends as dogs, cats, and horses, could people work up much sympathy for those forms of sentient life which they had decided were vermin—the woodchuck, the English sparrow, spiders and flies, the rattlesnake. The popular attitude was slightly different toward wild animals torn from their natural environment for human amusement.

Henry Bergh was a constant annoyance to Barnum in the latter's zoological activities, although Barnum usually extracted valuable publicity out of their clashes. An incident occurred when the A.S.P.C.A. learned that the boa constrictors in the Broadway menagerie were being fed living animals in the presence of paying customers. The resulting pressure from Bergh was so heavy that at one time Barnum had to send his snakes to Hoboken to feed them, beyond the reach of the A.S.P.C.A., whose writ did not run in New Jersey.

Barnum found a way to punish Bergh. He obtained from Agassiz a letter saying that snakes required live food and expressing doubt that the active members of the A.S.P.C.A. "would object to eating lobster salad because the lobster was boiled alive, or refuse oysters because they were cooked alive, or raw oysters because they must be swallowed alive." The president of Barnum & Van Amburgh's Museum and Menagerie thereupon demanded an apology from the president

CONTINUED ON PAGE 94

Now that you are Married, do not always expect the Lover

We are not sure exactly what it is that married women tell their little sisters about marriage nowadays, but it is certainly not very much like the letter we publish here. It was written in a spidery hand from a home on the newly settled upper Mississippi to a young bride, Mrs. Oliver Ormerod, back in Liverpool, England, and the advice it gives says more than any long treatise about the apologetic, indeed timorous, position of women only a century and a half ago. Mrs. Ormerod was the great-grandmother of our editor. She appears at left in an old miniature about the time she married her Anglican minister, and before she reared a large family of sons.

Prestons Retreat, Carrollton
February 6th, 1838

God bless you My dear little Sister, and may you ever be as happy as when you wrote the letter I have just received. It is a cold day in February & sitting by the fire writing to Mary & thinking of you all, the box was brought in containing your wedding cake & letter. My heart beats with love & my eyes are filled with tears of joy as I thank you for your kind remembrance. Oh, dearest, ever be watchful to guard your good husband's heart—I am sure I should love him because he knows how to prize you & it was affectionate in him to write even a few lines—but now that you are married, do not always expect the lover. Be more than ever anxious to please, study his interest, make it yours. If any little domestic care troubles you, such as indifferent servants &tc let it not ruffle your temper. Is it not better to endure this than wear him by not being amiable?

We undergo soon after marriage a trying change in our constitutions. We feel cross because we feel badly & scarcely know what ails us—not one gentleman in ten can make allowances for our peevish fits. Now dear if you ever feel them, conquer it, & be only what you seemed to be when first you won his love. Be more cautious of wounding the feelings of a husband than you were ever anxious to please the lover. If you are fond of any amusement he does not approve & cannot share, give it up—you will find your reward in so doing. You are to keep him happy & cheerful & to make sacrifices if necessary without murmur-ing. You may see faults in him that in your fondness you never dreamed of. Be as blind to them as you can. If by gentleness & love you cannot alter them, then conform yourself to your circumstances, for reproaches never will do good. Better feel the secret pain than let him fear you love him less than when you thought him faultless. Should you be blessed with children consider well what a responsible being you are.

I wish we had known whilst in New York that your husband had friends there. What a gratification it would have been to me to tell them how dear a little wife he had won.... I have taken it for granted that your husband is an Episcopalian. I have not yet seen Mr. Grimshaw to ask him. I look forward to your crossing the Atlantic some of these days. When once at New York it is nothing to go to Pitsburg [sic], & the floating hotels on the great Mississippi will bring you most speedily & pleasantly to our home. What rejoicing we should have! Frank, our son not yet seven, would amuse you much—he is a great rhymer & fond of punning. Robert Layton sixteen months old is a great beauty.

You have a Parson, Mary a soldier, & I a lawyer. Thank Ned for his few lines. My kindest love to Mother, Father and to your husband—as well as to all my brothers & sisters.

I shall ride down to see Mrs. Grimshaw as [soon] as the roads are good enough. I like her very much—there is a nameless something about her that always reminds me of Mary. Now, dear, accept the sincere wishes of your sister for your health & happiness.   Catherine Lawn Preston

*Forty years ago, American Marines
tangled with a tough Latin-American guerrilla
leader whose tactics against
"the capitalists" would evoke an unhappy shock
of recognition in Vietnam today*

Augusto Sandino in 1929

MR. COOLIDGE'S JUNGLE WAR

By RICHARD O'CONNOR

The United States was first introduced to the vexations of large-scale guerrilla warfare forty years ago in the mountain jungles of Nicaragua. There for the first time Americans were confronted by an elusive partisan leader of a type to become bitterly familiar not only in the Caribbean but in Southeast Asia, a man who pioneered techniques of warfare when Che Guevara and Fidel Castro were in rompers and Mao Tse-tung was an obscure revolutionary. "Mr. Coolidge's War," the affair has been called. More formally, it was the American intervention in Nicaragua of 1927–28—and though it was not one of the thunderclaps of history, its significance is evident.

For well over a year a particularly agile and mischievous guerrilla chieftain named Sandino—the name became almost a household word in the late twenties—campaigned successfully against the elite battalions of the United States Marine Corps. In giving them so much trouble, he unintentionally made his country a proving ground for U.S. weapons and tactics. In Nicaragua the Marine Corps began to formulate the doctrine that would guide the jungle campaigns against the Japanese in World War II and against the Viet Cong in South Vietnam; it tried out such novelties as dive-bombing, aerial support of ground forces, search-and-destroy missions, and the counterambush. It would not be appropriate to belabor the point, but with a change of dateline many of the dispatches from Vietnamese battlefields read like the afteraction reports of the Marines' provisional brigade in Nicaragua.

Similarly interchangeable would be the protests of liberal and pacifist elements in the United States. President Coolidge had his Senator Fulbright in the liberal Republican William E. Borah of Idaho, who kept demanding to know the true casualty figures of the U.S. force and of those opposed to it. Another senator introduced a resolution that would have forbidden the President to employ military forces when "Congress has not declared a state of war to exist." Hundreds of ordinary citizens picketed the White House with signs reading "Wall Street and not Sandino is the Real Bandit," and Marines bound for Nicaraguan duty received letters urging them to desert when they landed and join Sandino in his "war for freedom."

It was not primarily Wall Street's interests, nor any fervor for foreign ventures on the part of the lackadaisical Coolidge, nor even an ironclad interpretation of the Monroe Doctrine that propelled the intervention. For almost a century the United States had considered Nicaragua strategic to the national interest: it offered the best alternative route for a trans-Isthmus canal—a route that is still a matter of consideration in the event that political upheaval, or the need for a larger canal, should make an alternative to the Panama Canal necessary.*

This continuing strategic interest, plus the concessions obtained by American companies for the exploitation of Nicaragua's bananas, mahogany, and gold, made the country almost an American protectorate. Between 1912 and 1925, Marines were landed several times to restore order after political disturbances. The closely drawn struggle between the Liberal and the Conservative parties in Nicaragua, which had been going on since early in the nineteenth century, erupted with even greater violence late in 1926 when a Conservative, Adolfo Díaz, was elected to the presidency by the Nicaraguan congress and recognized by the United States and most of the other great powers. The Liberal leader, Dr. Juan Sacasa, then proclaimed himself president, with the support of revolutionary forces under General José Maria Moncada. Mexico recognized Sacasa and sent him four shiploads of arms and supplies. Before long, his forces had occupied large sections of the country.

former Secretary of War Henry L. Stimson to the embattled country aboard a cruiser just as General Moncada's revolutionary forces advanced to within forty miles of Managua, the capital.

Colonel Stimson briskly set about negotiating a truce between the contending factions. He persuaded President Díaz to offer the rebels a general amnesty, the return of confiscated property, and participation in the Díaz cabinet by Liberal leaders. Then Stimson arranged a meeting with General Moncada, which was held on May 4, 1927, under a large blackthorn tree just outside the village of Tipitapa. A week later they met there again. As a result, Moncada agreed to allow Díaz to stay in the presidency provided that the United States would supervise the election the following year.

The various rebel commanders, as requested, signed an agreement with General Moncada that they would surrender their arms—all but one, namely Augusto Sandino. The only word from Sandino was a note saying that he was going north to collect arms from his dissident followers and would "remain there await-

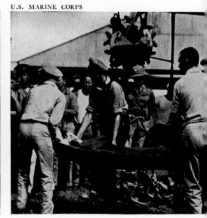

A welcoming arch waits in Nicaragua's capital; the Marines arrive, looking jaunty; soon after, the first wounded start back.

Once again the U.S. government felt it was necessary to intervene. The 5th Marine Regiment was landed on the Atlantic coast, and a shore party from the cruiser *Galveston* on the Pacific. The State Department gave the Associated Press a story pointing to the "spectre of a Mexican-fostered Bolshevistic hegemony intervening between the United States and the Panama Canal." By March of 1927 the U.S. Navy reported that 5,414 men were on duty in or en route to Nicaragua. However, President Coolidge decided to make a last try at a political solution. He rushed

ing your [Moncada's] orders." No one paid much attention to Sandino's absence as the various revolutionary battalions and the government forces surrendered their arms to officers of the 5th Marine Regiment. The job of policing the country was assumed by the Marines' provisional brigade and the Nicaraguan constabulary, which was to be commanded by Marine officers.

On May 15, Stimson confidently telegraphed the State Department: "The civil war in Nicaragua is now definitely ended. . . . I believe that the way is now open for the development of Nicaragua along the lines of peace, order, and ultimate self government."

The next day two Marines, Captain Richard B. Buchanan and Private Marvin A. Jackson, were killed

---

* A survey of the Nicaraguan route, undertaken by a commission set up by the U.S. Congress in 1938, estimated that such a canal would cost almost $1,500,000,000, against the $375,000,000 spent in Panama. Today, of course, it would cost much more.

when a guerrilla band attacked their post guarding the railroad near León.

Sandino had spoken. It was the starting gun of a long and bitter struggle to pacify the country. Stimson later recorded that General Moncada had told him that Sandino, "having promised to join in the settlement, afterward broke his word and with about 150 followers, most of whom he said were Honduran mercenaries, had secretly left his army and started northward toward the Honduras border."

Stimson left Managua that day, May 16, to return to Washington, convinced that Sandino and his band would soon be tracked down and captured. Instead, the Marine Corps, along with the Nicaraguan constabulary, found itself plunged into a guerrilla war with few guidelines and even fewer omens of success.

There were, to be sure, certain precedents. The Marines themselves had been engaged in police actions in Haiti. The U.S. Army, confronted on several occasions by guerrillas of various types, had learned and then forgotten the lesson that it takes a vast preponderance of men and materials to hunt down de-

Sandino, as Marine intelligence officers quickly learned, meant to stir up as much trouble as possible. He had taken his hard-core followers up into the heavily forested mountains of Nueva Segovia and Jinotega provinces near the Honduras border and was recruiting what became a striking force estimated at one thousand men. He had even designed a battle flag of red and black emblazoned with a death's-head. It was also observed that he was adept at rousing the patriotic emotions of the people in the back country by playing on resentment of foreign violations of their native soil, an emotion stronger in the mountains than in the more sophisticated cities to the south.

Augusto Sandino was a mestizo, not much over five feet tall, with a striking look of self-confidence in his intense black eyes. In 1927 he was thirty-four years old. The son of the owner of a small coffee plantation, he was educated at the Eastern Institute in Granada, worked on his father's *finca*, and then left his native Niquinohomo after a violent dispute with a prominent man in the vicinity. For a time he worked in

Sandino's rebels lay an ambush; line up for orders in a town under their control; and flaunt their death's-head ensign.

termined bands of partisans operating in rough country, among people friendly to the quarry but hostile to the hunters. During the Civil War the Union Army had been bedevilled by the irregular forces of Mosby, Quantrill, and others. In 1886 the regular Army had turned out 5,000 of its best troops to run down the Apache leader Geronimo and his followers, whose strength was approximately one per cent of their own. In the southern Philippines after the Spanish-American War, it had taken the army fourteen years to pacify the Moro *insurrectos*. An even more frustrating experience was General John J. Pershing's futile expedition into Mexico in 1916, chasing after Pancho Villa with the best of the U.S. Cavalry and coming back with an empty cage.

mines and on banana plantations in Nicaragua, and then he went to Mexico and was employed by an American oil company in Tampico. He returned to his father's home in 1926, laden with books on sociology and syndicalism—and, oddly enough, a bulky missionary tract, which he frequently consulted, published by the Seventh-day Adventists.

He loved to coin heroic slogans and hurl them at his followers on all suitable occasions ("Death is but one little moment of discomfort; it is not to be taken too seriously . . . God and our mountains fight for us"). But Sandino also had a sense of humor. Whenever he "requisitioned" supplies for his forces from the merchants, plantations, or mining companies on which he periodically descended, he insisted with sardonic punctilio on leaving nicely printed certificates: "The Honorable Calvin Coolidge, President of the United States of North America, will pay the bearer $——."

Sandino's objectives were succinctly stated in a message he left at the La Luz mines after levelling the American-owned property there: "The most honorable resolution which your government could adopt in the conflict with Nicaragua is to retire its forces from our territory, thus permitting us, the Nicaraguans, to elect our national government, which is the only means of pacifying the country. With your government rests the conservation of good or bad relations with our government and you, the capitalists, will be appreciated and respected by us according as you treat us as equals and not in the mistaken manner which now obtains, believing yourselves lords and masters of our lives and property."

The mordant edge of Sandino's humor was soon felt by Marine Captain G. D. Hatfield, whose force of thirty-seven Marines and forty Nicaraguan constables occupied Ocotal, the largest town in the province of Nueva Segovia, and formed the spearhead of the

where Sandino had worked as a clerk just before joining the Liberal revolution.

On July 15, on orders from his superiors, Captain Hatfield sent Sandino an ultimatum demanding that he surrender within twenty-four hours or be wiped out. "I will not surrender," Sandino replied, "and will await you here. I want a free country or death."

Actually he had already decided against "awaiting" the Marines in the mountains above Ocotal and had begun deploying for an attack. One day after receiving the ultimatum, at 1 A.M. on July 16, he launched a furious assault on the garrison at Ocotal with an estimated six hundred followers. Only luck saved Captain Hatfield and his men from destruction. A Marine sentry patrolling one hundred yards from the city hall sighted a shadow moving along a line of bushes. The shadow, startled, fired on him. The Marine raced to the city hall, where Hatfield's headquarters were located, and the town's defenders were alerted just before Sandino struck in force. The Sandinistas had infiltrated the town and were closing in on the main defense positions around the city hall.

Air power comes to the jungle: Marine aviators prepare to take off; a Fokker attempts an airdrop; a message is picked up.

forces charged with running down the rebel. Captain Hatfield and Sandino exchanged a number of letters inviting each other to surrender or, failing that, to "come out and fight." Sandino easily outdid the Marine commander in bravura. One of his messages was decorated with a drawing of a guerrilla brandishing a machete over the prostrate form of a Marine; it was signed, "Your obedient servant, who wishes to put you in a handsome tomb with flowers." Meanwhile, Sandino was striking hard at foreign-owned mining properties in the northern mountains. The managers of French and German mines near Ocotal were kidnapped and held for $5,000 ransom. Sandino and his followers also wrecked the gold mine operated by Charles Butters, an American, at San Albino,

Outnumbered by almost ten to one, the Marines and the constables reacted with admirable discipline and poured rifle, grenade, and machine-gun fire on the attackers from the rooftops, courtyards, and windows. One group of Sandino's men charged into the courtyard behind the city hall and killed a Marine, but was forced to withdraw. In the square fronting on Hatfield's command post, the partisans were caught in a crossfire between Marines in the city hall and the Guardia (constabulary) in the nearby church tower. Thomas G. Bruce, a Marine first sergeant commissioned as a lieutenant in the Guardia, lay in the street behind a heavy machine gun and accounted for many of the Sandinistas trying to cross the square.

At dawn, Sandino realized his surprise attack had

CONTINUED ON PAGE 89

William D. T. Travis

*Concerned lest history
overlook their triumphs,
veterans of the Army
of the Cumberland had them
writ large—on a canvas
five hundred feet long*

By BRUCE CATTON

Bill. D. T. Travis!

Is on his Seventh Annual Lecturing Tour, and will be here to present his GREAT NATIONAL

PAINTINGS!

A GRAND OFFICIAL PORTRAITURE OF THE

CUMBERLAND ARMY

Used to Illustrate His Historical Lectures on the Rebellion.

At _____

On_____ Eve., _____

The Whole Work Consisting of the

GRANDEST DISPLAY OF NATIONAL CARTOONS

Ever Presented

Sketched by MR. TRAVIS while the Scenes were being enacted, and painted by his own hand on a Capital of $4,000, furnished him by Cumberland Generals. This is no Magic Lantern, Peep Show or Panorama, but Large National Paintings on Canvass, each Scene 9 by 16 feet. The Press throughout the Country speaks in glowing terms of MR. TRAVIS' Lecture and Paintings.

THRILLING AND AMUSING SCENES,

CAMPS, HOSPITALS AND BATTLES.

Endorsed by all the Leading Newspapers.

Don't Fail to See It.

PROGRAMME.

Part First of Illustrations.	Part Second of Illustrations.
Going to the War,	Crossing the Tennessee on Pontoone,
General Rosecrans and Heroes,	Ascent of Sand Mountain, "Scenes of Beauty,"
Battle of Perryville, (Two Scenes,)	Little River Falls, (On Lookout Mountain,)
Burning R. R. Bridge at Nashville, Tenn.,	Ascent of Lookout Mountain, (from the
Camp Scene at Nashville Tennessee,	Broomtown Valley,
Forage Train Attack,	Battle of Chicamauga, (4 Scenes,)
Emancipation, (A Laughable Scene,)	Lookout Mountain, (from Chattanooga,
Battle of Stone River, (Three Scenes,)	Hazen's Flotilla at Brown's Ferry,
Forage Scenes, (Highly Humorous,)	Battle of Wauhatchie Valley,
Field Hospital at Murfreesboro,	Battle of Lookout Mountain,
Capture of Shelbyville,	R. R. Bridge over Falling Water,
Battle of Liberty Gap,	Battle of Mission Ridge,
Cavalry Raid on Franklin, Tenn.,	Two Equestrian Groups.

Our Special Artist mounted on his Noble Charger—BIG FOOL!

Greatest HORSE Paintings of the Age!!

Of which GEORGE D. PRENTISS said: "His work is the work of a fine brain and a skillful hand. Neither in Europe or America have I seen any Horse Painting equal to the Great Horse Painting Mr. TRAVIS has produced in his portraiture of the Cumberland. He is a Master.

SCENES OF RARE BEAUTY.

WHAT THEY SAY OF HIM:

GENERAL ROSECRANS pronounces him "unrivalled in his great conceptions of struggles on the Battle Field."

MAJOR GENERAL THOMAS said: "Young TRAVIS stands forth as a rival to the greatest masters of the day. His renderings are truly wonderful, so void of extravagance, so bound to the reality."

After MAJOR GENERAL D. S. STANLEY and his wife had visited the young Artist in his studo, the General wrote: "MR. TRAVIS certainly has the power to paint Battles very like reality."

MAJOR GENERAL L. H. ROUSSEAU said: MR. TRAVIS is a young man in whom I feel the deepest interest, because I regard him as one of the greatest artists now living."

Many more compliments have thus been paid the artist, but the above are enough. He shows one painting alone worth more than the price of admission—*Group of Horses*—acknowledged by the finest judges to be the best in the world. ☞ LET NONE FAIL TO SEE IT.

OLD LOOKOUT MOUNTAIN IN ALL HIS GRANDEUR !

MR. TRAVIS AND HIS WORKS.

Thousands have been delighted with his Sketches and Writings in the New York Illustrated papers. He now gives all a chance to see his *Original Portraiture* of the Cumberland, and hear one of his most singular *Historical Lectures*. Professors and Clergymen pronounce him an Orator of the strangest powers known in the Country. He is certainly possessed of a wonderful versatality of genius.

NOTE FROM MR. TRAVIS.—I wish to say to my Countrymen, and all kindly disposed Foreigners, that nothing short of my sincere gratitude can be given for any support I may receive from you, to aid me, in this noble aim of life. While I shall strive harder day by day to make myself worthy of you as best I can, my highest earthly ambition shall be that I may yet be claimed as

"YOUR OWN AMERICAN ARTIST"

☞ None should fail to see this great work of art which is endorsed by Thomas, Rosecrans, Stanley, Rousseau and other leading Generals who took part in the scenes and battles it depicts.

Admission 35 Cents. - - - - Children 25 Cents.

Doors open at 7 1-2 o'clock ; Lecture commences PROMPTLY at 8 1-2.

Bill. D. T. Travis is the Special Artist who did justice to the Subordinate Officers and Soldiers, in his Publications in "Harper's Weekly" and N. Y., "Illustrated News."

The Army of the Cumberland was one of the principal Union armies in the Civil War, and it was about as good an army as this country ever had. Its soldiers thought very well of themselves, which is one way of saying that it was a high-morale outfit, and they also thought very well of their generals, especially of the one who led them through a couple of the worst battles any army ever had: Major General William S. Rosecrans, a red-faced, excitable, hard-fighting man who was known to his troops as "Old Rosy." Rosecrans was a good man but unlucky. He lost a big battle, got into the bad graces of General U. S. Grant, and was removed from his command. As an indirect result, he and the army wound up with an unusual memorial in the form of a huge strip of painted canvas 500 feet long, eight feet high, and now

more than a century old, some scenes from which are shown here and on the pages immediately following.

First, a word about the Army of the Cumberland itself. It cut its eyeteeth in the fearful Battle of Shiloh in the spring of 1862, fought the hard and indecisive Battle of Perryville, Kentucky, that fall, and at the end of the year engaged in a terrible battle at Stones River, Tennessee. Then, in September, 1863, the army got into an even worse battle at Chickamauga, suffering a severe defeat and retiring to Chattanooga to stand a siege. It was at this time that General Grant removed Rosecrans and replaced him with George H. Thomas.

Two months later the army atoned for its defeat by breaking the siege and, with the help of General William T. Sherman's Army of the Tennessee, driving its Confederate opponents off Lookout Mountain and

The Travis panorama begins, properly enough, with this traditional scene showing the Army of the Cumberland on its way to war, with a gallant officer saying good-bye in the foreground. The pillared mansion, the log cabin, and the distant mountains indicate that the setting for this picture may have been in Kentucky.

Missionary Ridge and forcing them to retreat to Dalton, Georgia. Sherman's victorious campaign to Atlanta followed in the spring and summer of 1864, and that fall the Army of the Cumberland returned to Tennessee, beat a Confederate army at the battles of Franklin and Nashville, and insured permanent Federal control of the war in the West.

But the defeat at Chickamauga and the removal of Rosecrans had remained a sore spot with the army's veterans, and after the war they commissioned an artist to record their achievements on canvas.

The artist was William D. T. Travis, who had accompanied the army as a staff artist for *Harper's Weekly* and the New York *Illustrated News*. Working from his own on-the-spot sketches and his memories, Travis painted a huge panorama—thirty-two scenes on a long roll of canvas, which was arranged on two huge spindles for lecture-hall display.

When this ponderous work was finished, Travis and his younger brother James went on tour with it and displayed it all across the Middle West, the region from which most of the Cumberlands came. For a number of years the panorama was a great success. Then, when everybody who wanted to see it had seen it and had rejoiced in the recognition that had been given to the army, the bulky roll was retired to an attic in the big farmhouse that Travis used as home and studio in

Burlington, New Jersey. There it reposed for decades.

A subsequent owner of house and painting is a nephew of the artist, Mr. C. C. Travis, a businessman of Grand Rapids, Michigan. Mr. Travis felt that the present generation would enjoy seeing this "Portraiture of the Cumberland Army," and several years ago he got in touch with the editors of AMERICAN HERITAGE. Two of them went to Burlington and spent an afternoon in the dusty, almost airless attic, unwinding the cumbersome roll from its spindles and growing more and more enthusiastic, despite the heat and the dust, as they looked at the separate frames. Reproductions of some of these were made and used in the AMERICAN HERITAGE *Picture History of the Civil War;* now an assortment is presented in this magazine.

In the unfurling panorama, Travis set out to tell the story of the army he had lived with so long. He worked in battle scenes (at which, of course, he had been present), details of camp life, and incidents of the march and of foraging expeditions. In the end he produced a record that is both historically valuable and artistically charming.

To Mr. C. C. Travis our thanks are due for bringing the panorama to our attention. The huge canvas, by the way, no longer rests in dusty obscurity in the Burlington attic; it is now in the Museum of History and Technology of the Smithsonian Institution.

Above, Confederate troops evacuate Nashville, Tennessee, in February, 1862, burning a bridge to delay the advance of the Army of the Cumberland. The large panorama segment at left represents a dramatic moment in the Battle of Perryville, in the fall of 1862; a Union officer rallies his troops to meet an assault by the Confederate General Benjamin Cheatham's forces. Below is Travis' portrayal of one of the crowded Union hospitals that came into being at Murfreesboro, Tennessee, early in 1863, after the Battle of Stones River.

The great fight at Stones River was one of the most desperate of all the battles of the Civil War, and on this page Travis provides two glimpses of it. Above, his hero General Rosecrans (using field glasses, in the mounted group at the right) comes up to the front, as he so often did, and draws cheers from his men; below, a Federal battle line gives way before the fury of a Confederate charge. During the first day of this inconclusive fight, Rosecrans' army escaped defeat by a narrow margin.

44

How could this happen?

Months after the desperate Battle of Stones River, Rosecrans led his army on a skillful maneuver that forced the Confederates to evacuate Chattanooga. Above, Travis shows the army crossing the Tennessee River near Stevenson, Alabama, late in the summer of 1863, with Rosecrans in the foreground. Moving south after taking Chattanooga, the army met its one defeat at Chickamauga late in September of that year; a hand-to-hand struggle at one stage of that battle is shown below.

Not all of Travis' paintings depict combat action. Above, Union foragers seize pigs and chickens from a Southern farm; at left, the guards for a Union forage train presumably laden with spoils from just such an operation beat off an attack by avenging Confederates. At the upper right on the facing page is an engaging glimpse of camp life, with a rigid sentry strutting by while lesser mortals prepare a dinner. Below this there is a picture that Travis called, simply, "Emancipation"—a Tennessee manor house with the slaves running away, following the bright gleam that for them was represented by the battle-tried Army of the Cumberland.

It ended as it began, in blood and fire and human suffering, with young men daring more than they had thought they could face and, at last, doing more than anyone could have imagined. This picture shows Travis' rendering of the Battle of Lookout Mountain—the fabulous, half-unreal fight that took place late

in November of 1863, when the army stormed the frowning height that overlooked Chattanooga, breaking the left end of the supposedly invulnerable Confederate line and going on to win the victory that made final triumph secure. The painting of course is unreal . . . yet real enough, too, for later generations.

In the early days of the century, a fearless cowboy named Bill Pickett roused audiences on two continents by giving the fledgling sport of rodeo one of its most exciting events

He took

Bulldogger Bill Pickett and his reliable horse, Spradley, once pursued a wild steer into the audience at Madison Square Garden.

Ask nearly any American today to define the word *bulldogging* and he'll do a pretty fair job. So, for that matter, will many Europeans. But even as recently as the late 1800's, *rodeo* was still not much more than a Spanish word meaning *roundup,* and *bulldogging* was a term familiar only to a select group—people who knew Bill Pickett.

Pickett was a lonely man whose dark skin came from a Choctaw mother and a white-Negro-Indian father. Long a footloose cowhand, he had worked ranches in South America and in the American Southwest; he was nearing forty when just before the turn of the century he met Zack Miller in Fort Worth, Texas. Miller was one of three brothers who owned the sprawling, burgeoning 101 Ranch in Oklahoma, situated on the Ponca Indian reservation at the confluence of the Salt Fork and Arkansas rivers.

Miller was a good judge of horses and cattle and of the men who worked them. He signed Pickett on. It was the beginning of a friendship that spanned more than thirty years; Zack came to regard Pickett as "the greatest sweat-and-dirt cowhand that ever lived —bar none," and those who saw him in action as a bulldogger came to regard him as a living legend.

The 101 had more than its share of top hands. Johnny Brewer could ride the saltiest of broncos; Jim Hopkins was a roper par excellence (once—dead drunk—he won a $500 steer-roping bet using a loop and casting style he had never tried before); Kurt Reynolds was a fine all-around cowboy. Pickett would have to prove himself, and he did so by bulldogging steers.

Pickett claimed to have originated the sport, and few have disputed it. Versions differ on how he learned and perfected his stunt, but there is little mystery about his technique. "The way Bill went at it," runs an account in one history of the 101 and its men, "he piled out of his saddle onto the head of a running steer, sometimes jumping five or six feet to tie on. He'd grab a horn in each hand [digging in

the bull by the horns

By JERROLD J. MUNDIS

with his boot heels to slow the animal down] and twist them till the steer's nose came up. Then he'd reach in and grab the steer's upper lip with his strong white teeth, throw up his hands to show he wasn't holding on any more, and fall to one side of the steer, dragging along beside him until the animal went down.

"Sometimes Bill would miss getting that tooth-hold. When he did, he'd just peg his steer by shoving the left horn into the ground, letting him roll, rump-over-head." But it was the biting of the steer's tender upper lip that turned the trick—and gave the sport its name.

Zack Miller recalled that he never saw a steer go after Pickett, once the animal had regained its feet. All Bill had to do, said Miller, was to stand his ground. It was all most impressive.

Pickett soon was putting his talent to good use. On some days there was time to spare, and cowpunchers from two or three outfits would get together to compete for small purses or personal bets. It was at these informal range meets that, thanks to Pickett, the sport of bulldogging began to spread. The 101 hands promoted many winning bets on Pickett; moreover, his specialty was irresistibly exciting. Others began hurling themselves onto the backs of half-wild Texas longhorns; there were several cases of broken bones, but few of diminished enthusiasm. The meets grew in popularity and were soon scheduled regularly. The purses increased—and so did the distances men would ride to vie for them.

Never one to miss an opportunity, Zack Miller staked his men to entrance fees and travel money—all he asked was fifty per cent of whatever prize money they pulled down. The 101 boys won so consistently that by 1900, hands from other spreads were branding the Miller employees professionals, outlawing them from the competitions. Zack shrugged, and his cowboys went back to the routine of running the ranch.

And the ranch was prospering. The 101 had at-

A stylized depiction of the Pickett method of bulldogging adorned this program for the Miller brothers' wild West show.

There's been Bull Riding on TV

51

tracted the eyes of dudes and easterners, and was fast becoming a favorite spot for western holidays. The booming tourist trade was mainly attributable, of course, to the 101's stuntmen-in-residence. Doubtless many a tenderfoot returned to the East with spellbinding accounts of how a Negro cowboy, right before his very eyes, had barehandedly wrestled to earth a mean steer with a horn-spread—well, it was *this big!*

Pickett by this time was an integral part of the ranch. He no longer carried with him the vague sense of emptiness that had been so constant a companion in his peripatetic earlier days. The 101's crew comprised men much like himself, men who understood and respected each other. He had a home now, he had friends, and he liked it.

One of Pickett's pals was an easygoing young fellow named Will Rogers. Rogers was never a regular hand at the 101. He'd drift in, work for as long as he liked, and then drift on again, but he was an exceptionally good worker, and the arrangement suited Zack. At the 101, Rogers perfected a number of rope-twirling tricks that shortly earned him a trip to New York.

In the fall of 1904, Zack hired a good-looking French-Canadian-Italian from behind a bar in Oklahoma City. If they could make a half-decent cowboy out of him, Zack thought, he'd be just the man to entertain the dudes. Some of the hands had to saddle his horse for him a time or two, but soon Tom Mix was handy enough with a rope and horse to convince any tourist he had been at it all his life. Mix took his place next to the other experts at the 101: he was the greatest teller of tall tales they'd ever heard. He could ramble for hours about his crucial part in winning the Boer War, about his exploits as a Texas Ranger, about his childhood as the adopted son of a Comanche chief—and about how he'd taught Bill Pickett the proper way to bulldog a steer. Zack said Mix could color a story redder than a Navajo blanket.

In February of 1905 Zack met J. L. Gue, a promoter for an annual horse fair at Madison Square Garden in New York. Gue was looking for a gimmick to increase gate receipts. Zack handed him a cigar, started talking as Gue was lighting up, and a few hours later walked away with a signed contract.

Zack and two dozen of his best hands—Pickett and Rogers among them—made the trip East. Gue had arranged for them to put up at a swanky Fifth Avenue hotel, but when its manager insisted that they wear coats and ties to dinner, Zack told him, "Why, me 'n' the boys had rather eat in a stable than dress up like show monkeys for a chance to eat in that damned dining room of yours."

Gue hastened to smooth the ruffled feathers. Soon he moved the noisy crew into the Putnam House; it

Zack Miller, who with his brothers George and Joe owned the 101 Ranch that made Pickett and his specialty famous, is pictured here in a show program.

was nearer the Garden, and the management turned the whole place over to them. This was more like it: here they could (and did) whoop it up; soon they worked out a room-buzzer code with the bellhops—a hand could get the drink of his choice just by buzzing so many times.

The Garden's opening-night crowd was small, but none among it ever forgot the performances of Bill Pickett and Will Rogers.

At one end of the arena Pickett was mounted on Spradley, a four-year-old he had nursed back to health when as a colt it had driven a large splinter into its chest. To his right was Rogers, ready to ride haze. Between them was a closed chute.

The chute's gate banged open, and a large Texas longhorn shot out. Pickett and Rogers shot after it. At full speed the animal headed straight for the high, closed gate at the opposite end of the arena. Spradley couldn't cut down the distance, and Pickett figured he'd make the catch when the longhorn turned. But it didn't turn. Into the air it went, splintering the top boards of the gate, and into an aisle that led up into the first balcony of the grandstand. Spradley cleared the gate without breaking stride; close behind was Rogers, no longer an effective hazer, but a more than interested onlooker.

Spectators scrambled over each other as the bellowing steer, two horses, and two shouting cowboys clattered upward—to the third tier, where Pickett left the saddle and hit the steer just as Rogers snaked his lariat over its hind legs. Pickett hung on to the animal's horns while Rogers dragged and bumped the protesting renegade back down into the arena.

For the remainder of the engagement the houses were good, although it was said that aisle seats were less in demand than usual. Gue's show had made money for the first time in years; he hired a special coach with an open bar for the riders' train trip home.

Early that summer the 101 was the convention site of the National Editorial Association. The climax of the week-long fete was a gala western spectacular—Indians, ropers, marksmen, riders, and a mock attack on a covered-wagon train—all of it open to the public. Regional newspapers had publicized the event months in advance, but still the Millers were astounded—64,000 people showed up for the big day. If people were that hungry for an authentic touch of the West, Zack and his brothers were ready to feed them.

The 101 Wild West Show opened in Kansas City in the spring of 1906, and by the time the seventy-five-man troupe returned to the ranch for the winter, the show was a solidly established success. It netted $30,000 in a single week, playing to record crowds at the Chicago Coliseum in 1907, and from there it went to Jamestown, Virginia, for a 100-day run. Profits soared in 1908, and advance ticket offices were sold out weeks before the troupe arrived. The Millers were riding high.

The wild West show hit Mexico City one night in mid-December, 1908. A few days later Pickett, then forty-seven years old, risked his life in El Toreo, the new steel and concrete bullring, in one of the strangest combats in the chronicles of the West.

The Mexicans were critical of the 101 show, and looked upon the *norteamericanos* with contempt and distaste. Pickett drew particularly heavy fire. His act was vulgar and disgusting, said an editorial in *El Heraldo,* and the man himself lacked the dignity, the grace, and the courage of a matador. The Miller brothers responded by offering a thousand pesos for Mexican charity if there was a single bullfighter in the city who could pull off Pickett's stunt.

Bienvenida, a popular matador, accepted the wager and the time was agreed upon. *El Heraldo* devoted three columns to the event, smugly predicting that Bienvenida would "teach the boasting Americans a lesson in grace and courage."

The day and time came—and went. The Millers sent a man to Bienvenida's quarters. The messenger returned with a note from the matador: his backers had advised him that it would be demeaning to participate in such a crude and barbaric spectacle. But they had an alternative proposition. They would pay $5,000 if Pickett, bare-

handed, would take on a fighting bull in the arena.

The Millers—and Pickett—quickly accepted this challenge, although there were certain rather ugly stipulations. Pickett was to fight without benefit of *picadors,* the mounted lancemen who take the bull's first charges and tire it, or *banderilleros,* who weaken the bull's shoulders with barbed shafts. Bill was to remain in the ring for fifteen minutes; although he would not be required to down the bull, he would have to maintain direct physical contact with it for five consecutive minutes.

On the day of combat, 25,000 Mexicans packed El Toreo. Among them were President Porfirio Díaz and other dignitaries who came, as *El Heraldo* put it, to watch Bill Pickett "sacrifice himself on the altar of American egotism."

In the pre-performance parade that afternoon, local matadors carried a coffin upon which was inscribed *El Pincharino,* fairly translated as "one who has been gored through." There was little question in the minds of the spectators as to what the outcome would be; it was strictly a matter of time. Local bookmakers, it was said, were giving Pickett four minutes.

The bull selected was a tough, experienced fighter that had been spared by an admiring crowd because of his good performance in the ring a week earlier. He was called Chiquito Frijole, "Little Bean," because of his oddly speckled skin.

The Millers had expected to give their regular wild West show that day, with Pickett's act as the grand finale. But the mood of the crowd was all too apparent. They were not willing to wait. *"El Pincharino!"* they shouted. *"Chiquito Frijole!" "Viva el toro!"*

As for Bill Pickett, he was ready. Not that he was unaware of the mortal danger. The night before, Pickett had come to Zack Miller asking for a promise.

The Millers' wild West shows had tremendous appeal, even when they were presented at the 101 itself. This picture is undated, but an automobile buff could tell that they were still packing them in during the mid-twenties.

If he died out there in that Mexican bullring, he said, he wanted his body taken back to the 101 Ranch and buried in good, hard ground where the coyotes could not "scratch out his bones." Zack had given his word.

Pickett's heels touched Spradley, and the horse moved forward. At the far side of the arena a gate opened, and into the sunlight charged Chiquito Frijole. A great thunder rolled up from the crowd: *"Muerte al Negro de Oklahoma!"*

The bull did not wait for the fight to come to him: he dug at the sand and snorted, head twisting, and then began his charge. Pickett held the reins loosely; Spradley, well enough versed in mean animals, did a dancing step, marking time, waiting for the bull to come. Chiquito Frijole's head dropped, his horns ready to disembowel. At the last instant Spradley side-stepped, and the bull rushed past.

The bull refused to maintain a straight line, and as Spradley pursued him, he wheeled—again the horse had to dodge. Spradley's footwork kept him out of danger, but Pickett had no opportunity to engage the beast. When Chiquito Frijole overshot twice again, Pickett turned and rode to the barricade.

The rider was worried because he now realized he would have to present a stationary target—his horse—to lure the bull into position. "A pony's gonna die before I can get close enough," he called to the Miller brothers. "I can't risk my Spradley horse."

"Cobarde!" screamed the crowd, thinking Pickett was conceding defeat. The impresario rose, reached for his handkerchief, and pointed at Pickett.

"Go back in there, Bill, and get that bull," urged Zack. "If you don't, they're going to get all of us!"

Pickett, face twisted, jerked the reins and galloped out again. Chiquito Frijole barrelled forward, and Pickett drew Spradley up short. The horse screamed as the bull's horns pierced its hind quarters. As the bull pulled back for another thrust, Pickett left the saddle and slid backward over Spradley's rump and onto the bloody horns. Dragging Pickett, Chiquito Frijole made straight for Spradley, but the limping pony escaped through a hastily opened gate.

Bill Pickett had a rough ride. His antagonist raced across the arena, head high and tossing. Bill jammed his heels into the ground—it had always slowed longhorns—to no avail. The bull, now throwing the cowboy against a wall, now on its knees trying to impale him against the arena's dirt floor, made Pickett abandon all thoughts of fancy, aggressive bulldogging. He just wanted to hang on. The bull whipsawed him like a rag doll.

Kurt Reynolds, leaning over the barricade, winced. "He can't last long," he shouted. "He's being murdered! How long has he been on?"

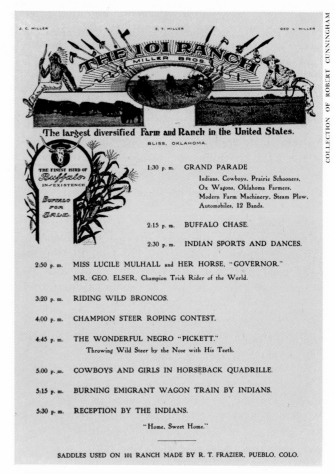

Above is the program of events for the final day of the National Editorial Association convention at the 101 in June of 1905. It is doubtful that anyone left before 5:00 P.M.

Zack glanced at his watch. "Two minutes."

Somehow, Pickett wrapped his arms around the bull's neck, locking his wrists under its throat. He pulled his legs up and squeezed his knees against the animal's nostrils. "The hold was Pickett's favorite," a member of the 101 said later, "and never before had a four-footed creature withstood it." The bull was weakening.

This was not at all what the crowd had come to see. A bottle glinted in the sunlight as it arched through the air, landing a few feet from the combatants. The crowd surged to its feet, screaming for blood. Bottles, cushions, and fruit cascaded down.

"Time!" cried Zack.

Chiquito Frijole pirouetted and whirled. Pickett, hugging the bull's head as if welded to it, was still choking off the animal's breath. The rain of debris continued.

"They're not going to ring that bell, Joe," yelled Zack to his brother. "The sons of bitches aim to let that bull kill Bill Pickett!"

The next few minutes were so tense, so confused, that afterward everyone had his own version of just what had happened. Zack Miller's memory was that Joe shouted to an arena attendant to open the gate; Zack and some of his hands spurred through to rescue Pickett, two of them lassoing the bull's legs immediately. Someone else remembered that a cowboy ripped off his red shirt to distract the animal while Bill slipped off. Still another is said to have whipped out a skinning knife and sunk it in the bull's flank. At any rate, Pickett got away while the crowd raged murderously. President Díaz, fearful of mob action, ordered a troop of *rurales* to guard the cowboys; in fact, the 101 crew had a twenty-four-hour guard for its remaining few days in Mexico. Incredibly, Pickett's most serious injuries were three broken ribs and severe skin lacerations. Perhaps more incredible was the fact that the Millers collected on their bet.

The 101 Ranch and its wild West show became a part of the nation's vocabulary in the following decade. Zack and his cowboys performed coast to coast, from Canada to the Rio Grande. In 1914 the Millers received an invitation to the Anglo-American Exposition in London. The show was split, and Zack, with the prime half, stepped onto British soil on April 29. They played to record crowds, and one night had the honor of performing before King George V and Queen Mary. At one point, his Majesty became so excited that he broke into applause all by himself; the Queen, shocked at so flagrant a breach of royal etiquette, slapped the King's hands. Pickett's act was as popular in England as it was at home, and brought him an invitation to dine at the castle of an earl. Bill had a tough time figuring out when to use which pieces of flatware, and was just as happy to wind up the evening eating leftovers in the show's mess tent.

In October of 1914—some three months after Austrian Archduke Ferdinand was murdered at Sarejevo —the first peal of the show's death knell sounded. A royal courier delivered an official letter to Zack. In the top left corner were the words "National Emergency"; in the right, "Impressment Order Under Section 115 of the Army Act." The first paragraph began: "His Majesty having declared that a national emergency has arisen, the horses and vehicles of the 101 Ranch Show are to be impressed for the public service."

By the following week the show's animals, wagons, and stable gear had been confiscated for the British Army. Zack and his performers booked passage on the overloaded American mail ship *St. Paul,* along with seven hundred other Americans fleeing the war. The better part of the show had been left in England, and the possibility of America's entering the conflict diminished the popularity of the stateside remainder.

After two straight years of losses, the show was sold.

Bill Pickett was now fifty-five years old. Many of his old friends were gone, and the ranch itself had changed its personality, had grown too big and unwieldy. But when the war was over and good times followed, the Millers decided to try once more, and in April of 1925 a new and lavish 101 Touring Show opened in Oklahoma City with a roster of new stars like California Frank, Cotton Ashley, Buck Lucas, and Buff Brady. But, for all its color, it was doomed— by such formidable competition as Ringling Brothers and Sells-Floto, by top performers' demands for top salaries, by income taxes and lawsuits, by the deaths of George and Joe Miller in the late twenties, and finally by the Depression.

Rodeo, of course, survived the bleak and dispiriting thirties and remains a thriving institution. The 101 Ranch was not as hardy. Bankrupt, it was ordered liquidated by the District Court of Kay County, the sale of properties to begin on March 23, 1932. Zack Miller, recuperating from a nervous breakdown, filed a petition the day before the auction, and was given twenty-four hours to cut out his personal stock from the ranch's horses. Bill Pickett, seventy-one years old and now retired, had bought and stocked 160 acres near Chandler, Oklahoma. He visited the 101 occasionally, and did so now to help his friend.

On the morning of the twenty-third, Bill entered a corral, rope in hand, to cut out a skittish sorrel. He sailed the loop over the animal's head on the first toss. The horse backed to the fence and reared. Pickett climbed the rope hand over hand. Again the sorrel reared. Twenty-five years earlier the dark-skinned bulldogger would have scrambled easily to one side. But now a hoof struck his head and he fell to his knees, dazed, still clutching the rope. The horse rose and plunged, and Pickett's skull was fractured.

A doctor was rushed to the ranch, but could do nothing. Pickett hung on, unconscious, for eleven days. Zack Miller, against his own doctor's orders, maintained a bedside vigil until his old hand died.

Pickett was buried at the 101 atop a soapstone hill —in the hard ground he had requested so long before.

Zack wrote the epitaph for Pickett's headstone, an epitaph for a man who had given the nation one of its most exciting rodeo events, for the only man of the West ever known to brace a Spanish fighting bull with his bare hands, for an old friend.

It was the simply put sentiment of an aging, mournful man:

> He left a blank that's hard to fill
> For there'll never be another Bill.

Mr. Mundis is a free-lance writer living in New York.

Giacomo Beltrami's discoveries were mostly illusory,
but he had a glorious time making them, and the
people of Minnesota have never forgotten his name

THE PREPOSTEROUS PATHFINDER

By TIMOTHY SEVERIN

ILLUSTRATED FOR AMERICAN HERITAGE BY CHARLES B. SLACKMAN

In the serious story of the exploration of the Mississippi River, there is one unique and preposterous character. He is Giacomo Constantino Beltrami, an Italian of comic-opera proportions. Beltrami was in every way a glorious misfit. He was wayward, unpredictable, and humorous. It was impossible for him to be anything but a charming maverick, and when this dilettante set forth alone to discover the true source of the Mississippi, he did so in a gush of hyperbole. His account of his explorations, written in the form of letters to a friend, is bombastic and extravagant; a delightful note of absurdity runs through every page of Beltrami's adventures in the depths of Minnesota.

Beltrami was forty-two years old when he began what he described as his "pilgrimage." A citizen of the Venetian republic, he had been a vice-inspector of the army and a judge in the civil and criminal courts before he was exiled in 1821 as a political conspirator. Beltrami packed his bags on a mule and, like Don Quixote, set out to seek adventure as a "promeneur, solitary, unprotected, struggling by his unaided efforts with every sort of difficulty, privation and danger." Before he left, he promised to send back full reports to his old friend, the Countess Giulia Medici-Spada.

Determined during his exile to see and do everything expected of a gentleman-traveller, Beltrami began his pilgrimage with a Grand Tour of Europe. He poked and pried everywhere, and finally, on November 3, 1822, took ship for America from Liverpool.

Beltrami had a miserable passage across the Atlantic. He loathed ocean voyages and was violently seasick. Furthermore, because the regular packet service had its terminus in New York, and a yellow-fever epidemic was raging there, he had decided to go directly to Philadelphia aboard a small American merchant vessel. The change of route was a disaster. The ship's cook had deserted and the regular cabin steward was assigned to the galley. To replace the steward, an ordinary deckhand was detailed to look after the passengers. As a result, Beltrami noted, "the hour of dinner discovered . . . that we had neither steward nor cook." Later, conditions went from bad to worse. The cabin was filthy, the meat putrid, and the captain a drunken rogue. The newly appointed steward turned out to be a thief, and the food ran out. For weeks they were delayed by storms off the Irish coast. While the ship tossed and heaved, Beltrami clung to his bunk, refusing to eat the rotten fare and imploring the captain to put in to the nearest port. His fellow passengers, two Spanish Americans whom Beltrami firmly believed to be off-duty pirates, alternately prayed for salvation and raided the Italian's private stock of wines until it was all gone. Finally, after fist fights among the crew, gales, and near shipwreck, they reached Philadelphia; Beltrami thankfully scrambled ashore, convinced that he had narrowly escaped a most terrible death.

Once he was safely on dry land, the Italian's high spirits bubbled back. He "promenaded" briskly around Philadelphia and Baltimore, then moved on to Washington. There he inspected the Capitol and other public buildings, made comparisons to the senate of early Rome, and was immensely pleased to meet President Monroe in person. Travelling westward by stage coach and hired wagon, Beltrami continued his pilgrimage, carefully jotting down his impressions of the country: Kentuckians were "brave, industrious and active" but also "coarse and insolent," the roads "detestable," and Pittsburgh a "little Birmingham of the United States." Very little escaped his eye, and he did not hesitate to give personal opinions. He found that American women were superior to their menfolk, being "agreeable without forwardness, modest without affectation, well-informed without pedantry, and are excellent housewives," but he was not so enthusiastic about coeducational schools, where, he feared, "opportunity will prevail over the most austere principles."

By April 20, 1823, Beltrami had reached the confluence of the Ohio and the Mississippi rivers, intending to take a steamboat to New Orleans and then continue to Mexico. Quite by chance, the first boat to call was the *Calhoun*, bound for St. Louis, in the opposite direction. On board was Major Lawrence Taliaferro, an Indian agent assigned to Fort St. Anthony (later called Fort Snelling), an army post at the mouth of the Minnesota River. Beltrami seized on Taliaferro and bombarded him with questions about the north country. The Major's descriptions of the upriver Indians captivated the romantic Italian. Impulsively he threw over his plan to visit New Orleans and took passage on the *Calhoun*, determined to visit those tribes whose "extraordinary character had, from infancy, excited both my astonishment and my incredulity." Thus, in a fit of whimsy, Beltrami joined the ranks of Mississippi explorers.

Beltrami made a good river commentator. From the start he resolved to ignore "hydraulics, hydrometrics, hydrostatics, hydrodynamics, and a whole dictionary of such hard words . . . for all this is Greek to me." Instead, he was interested in Indians, pioneer figures, the scenery, and of course "antiquities." It was difficult to apply classical quotations to frontier America, but Beltrami tried hard. At St. Louis he put the Indian burial mounds in the same class as the Parthenon, Mithraic temples, and the pyramids of Giza.

Nothing could deflect Beltrami from his chosen role as a gentleman-traveller of grace and education. When he was not sauntering around the deck of the *Calhoun,* he was sweeping dandified bows to astonished frontier farmers' wives in their log cabins, and in St. Louis he minced happily through "a very brilliant ball, where the ladies were so pretty and so well dressed, that they made me forget I was on the threshold of savage life."

At St. Louis, Beltrami and Major Taliaferro transferred to the *Virginia.* It was to be a momentous trip. The *Virginia* was the first steamboat to attempt the upstream journey to Fort St. Anthony, and no one knew whether she would manage to battle through the rapids. Beltrami loved the drama of the venture. In great excitement he hung over the rail to watch the paddle wheel push the stubby vessel against the rushing water. Day by day he pestered the crew for details of the boat's progress. The *Virginia*'s captain was taking no chances and proceeded cautiously, so Beltrami had plenty of time to go ashore en route. Each sortie into the forest was an adventure. The Italian, draped with rifle, pistols, and sword, trod gingerly through the undergrowth, looking for a lurking savage behind every tree. He blazed away at wild turkeys, pondered on the beauty of nature, and managed to bag a rattlesnake. Of course Beltrami preserved the reptile's skin, for he was an inveterate souvenir hunter and was busily putting together a magpie collection of Americana that included tomahawks and dried Indian scalps.

The *Virginia* was having a rough trip, even without Beltrami's exaggerations. She hit a rock in the Des Moines rapids, luckily without puncturing her hull, and narrowly escaped a forest fire that threatened to engulf her. There were repeated delays while the crew cut firewood for the boilers or pulled their vessel off sand bars. The Italian did not complain; each halt was an opportunity for more exploring. On one excursion he lost his bearings and used his compass to return to the landing place only to find the boat gone. Imagining himself abandoned forever in the wilderness, Beltrami rushed frantically along the bank, firing his gun to attract attention. To his immense relief, the *Virginia* was just around the next bend, firmly aground on another sand bar.

To supplement the accounts of his excursions on shore, the Italian compiled notes on his fellow passengers. The prize exhibit was a Sauk chief named Great Eagle, who was returning from his first visit to St. Louis, where he had been presented with a military uniform to wear on the way home. To Beltrami's delight, the chief's first act on coming aboard the *Virginia* was to remove his uniform and strut around "in statu quo of our first parents." Great Eagle did not stay long. Exasperated by the steamer's slow progress, he dived into the river and swam to the bank. Next day he was waiting to greet the boat when she reached his encampment, and he came aboard to collect his belongings. Beltrami, still playing the tourist, shook him by the hand and persuaded him to sell a scalp lock that dangled from the handle of his war club. Another passenger who entertained his curiosity was a female missionary on her way to convert the savages. Evidently she was practicing on the ship's crew—with total lack of success. She was, Beltrami concluded, "one of those women who devote themselves to God when they have lost all hope of pleasing men." Passing his time with such gentle prattle in his reports to the Countess, Beltrami rode the steamer northward until the *Virginia* at last reached her destination, Fort St. Anthony, and the garrison unloaded her cargo of military supplies.

When Beltrami visited the upper river, the semi-savage conditions that Zebulon Pike had encountered in 1805 were much diluted. The army had moved into the area, a smattering of settlers had arrived and set up homesteads, and the Indian threat was more imaginary than real. Fort St. Anthony (a hundred and eighty miles upriver from Prairie du Chien, Wisconsin) was now the northern outpost of the white man's civilization. Beyond the fort the wilderness was still dominant. Poor soil, bad drainage, and an inhospitable climate discouraged immigrants, so the land was left to isolated bands of Sioux and Chippewa, who eked out a meager livelihood fishing, hunting, and trapping. The only real significance of this headwater region was its position as the frontier zone between the United States and Canada; this was enough to interest the American government in sponsoring further exploration of what is now upper Minnesota.

Beltrami's visit to Fort St. Anthony coincided with the arrival of an official American expedition under Major Stephen H. Long to define and map the line of the U.S.-Canadian border. This was a great stroke of luck for the wandering Italian. Normally he would have been turned back at the fort by its commandant, Colonel Snelling, who could not allow casual "tourists" to venture unescorted into tribal lands. As it was, Beltrami made friends with the Colonel and with Taliaferro's help managed to get himself attached unofficially to Long's expedition. The Italian was elated. He sent an exuberant letter to the Countess, sold his fine repeater watch to raise money to buy a horse and provisions, distributed presents to the Colonel and his family, and informed Long that he was ready to go. The Major—a gloomy and totally unimaginative man—was not pleased. He was running a military expedition under the auspices of the Department of War, and he did not relish the prospect of a civilian hanger-on. Long made his feelings brutally clear. He tried to dissuade Beltrami with descriptions of the dangers the expedition would encounter, the privations they would endure, and the expense of the trip for a private individual. Beltrami refused to be put off by Long's rudeness. His intention, he wrote, of "going in search of real sources of the Mississippi, was always before my eyes. I was therefore obliged to sacrifice my pride."

On the seventh of July the expedition, Beltrami included, left the fort and started up the Minnesota River. The party consisted of Major Long, a lieutenant, twenty-eight soldiers, an astronomer to determine their route, a zoologist, a professor of mineralogy and chemistry to take rock samples, and a landscape painter to help with the mapping and to draw pictures of Indian life. For guides they had Joseph Snelling, the Colonel's son, and Joseph Renville, one of the most famous frontiersmen in the northwest. Renville's mother was a full-blooded Sioux of good family, and the scout himself was highly respected by the Indians for his courage and tact. In the War of 1812, Renville had fought for the British and had risen to the rank of captain in the irregulars. Now he was working as an independent fur trader and guide. Naturally Beltrami was fascinated by the swashbuckling half-breed, who seemed to epitomize the courage and dash of the fearless Indian scout.

Unfortunately, although the trip went smoothly apart from one or two upsets in the Minnesota rapids, Beltrami was unhappy. The source of his troubles was his relationship with Major Long. The verbose Italian and the crisp West Pointer took an instant dislike to one another. Beltrami thought the soldier stupid and overbearing, and Long considered his supernumerary a trifler. There was constant bickering between them. Beltrami could not refrain from criticizing the management of the expedition, and Long naturally resented the Italian's interference. By the end of the first week even the pettiest frictions became insupportable. Beltrami complained that he was not being given his fair share of food from the common stock even though he had contributed generously at Fort St. Anthony, and he privately suspected that Long assigned him the wettest sleeping place in the tent whenever a thunderstorm was brewing over the camp. Matters finally came to a head when Beltrami and another man returned to camp after a hunting trip to learn that Long had failed to warn them of a threatened Indian attack. Beltrami was incensed and decided that he could no longer tolerate the Major. He decided to leave the expedition as soon as possible. Meanwhile, the party continued northward, now along the Red River.

Beltrami's chance to strike out on his own came when the expedition reached Pembina, the southernmost settlement of the Earl of Selkirk's colony in the Red River valley. This was a pioneer attempt at planned colonization in which Lord Selkirk, operating through agents, had induced European immigrants to start a new life on his lands. One of Long's tasks was to determine whether Pembina lay within the United States or Canada; from there he was under orders to proceed eastward to Lake Superior, moving well to the north of the Mississippi's headwaters. Up to this point Long had refused to tell Beltrami the exact path that the expedition had been following, but at Pembina, Beltrami knew that he was north and west of the Mississippi's source. He reasoned that if he worked his way back to the confluence of the Red and the Bloody (as he called the Red Lake River), and then followed the Bloody southeastward, he would reach the swampy region in which the Mississippi was known to rise. Accordingly, he sold his horse, hired an interpreter and two Chippewa Indians, and separated himself from Long's command, despite the "dangers which I was going to brave among the Indians, who are generally described as being very ferocious."

Although he was undoubtedly exaggerating the Indian menace, Beltrami had made a bold decision. The journey up the Red Lake River was not an easy task. The stream ran strong and there were numerous rapids, all of which had to be portaged knee-deep on the slippery rocks as the little group dragged its canoe forward. The interpreter turned back almost immediately, and Beltrami was left to communicate with the two Chippewa by gestures. At first the Indians behaved well, and Beltrami's little party made good progress. Then on August 14 they ran into trouble. The Chippewa were ambushed by a marauding band of Sioux, and although Beltrami escaped injury (the Sioux fled as soon as they saw his white skin), one of his guides was shot through the arm. The ambush gave the Chippewa a bad fright and they refused to go any farther by water lest the Sioux attack again. Beltrami tried to be firm, but it was useless. After a brief argument in sign language, the two Indians gathered up their belongings and decamped into the woods, leaving the Italian sitting disconsolately on the bank with his baggage and a canoe he did not know how to paddle. "I imagine, my dear Countess," he wrote, "that you will feel the frightfulness of my situation at this crucial moment more strongly than I can express it. I really can scarcely help shuddering . . . whenever I think of it."

According to his own version of that momentous day, Beltrami rose to the occasion magnificently. First he mused on the fate of Robinson Crusoe. Next he loaded his musket in case he had to defend himself against the white bears "which abound near the Red River" (and which, he stated, sustained themselves during their winter hibernation by sucking the fat from their paws). Then he resolved that at all costs he would continue his journey in search of the mysterious source. At that point his adventures took a comic turn, which he had the grace to describe:

I jumped into my canoe and began rowing. But I was totally unacquainted with the almost magical art by which a single person guides a canoe, and particularly a canoe formed of bark, the lightness of which is overpowered by the current, and the conduct of which requires extreme dexterity. Frequently, instead of proceeding up the river, I descended; a circumstance which by no means shortened my voyage. Renewed efforts made me lose my equilibrium, the canoe upset, and admitted a considerable quantity of water. My whole cargo was wetted. I leaped into the water, drew the canoe on land, and laid it to drain with the keel upwards. I then loaded it again, taking care to place the wetted part of my effects uppermost, to be dried by the sun. I then resumed my route.

For some hours this erratic progress continued, and, if we are to believe the incurably optimistic Italian, he was thoroughly amused by his efforts at paddling. Indeed, he told the Countess that he could "scarcely help incessantly smiling," even though it was quite obvious that he was making little or no headway.

Unabashed, he tried another means of locomotion:

I threw myself into the water up to my waist, and commenced a promenade of a rather unusual kind, drawing the canoe after me with a thong from a buffaloe's hide, which I had fastened to the prow. The first day of my expedition, the 15th of the month, was employed in this manner, and I did not stop till the evening. It was natural to expect that I should be fatigued; but I was not in the least so. While thus dragging after me my canoe, with a cord over my shoulder, an oar in my hand for my support, my back stooping, my head looking down, holding conversation with the fishes beneath, and making incessant windings in the river, in order to sound its depths, that I might most safely pass; I must leave to your imagination to conceive the variety and interest of the ideas which rapidly passed in review before my mind!

Despite the discomforts of his situation, Beltrami was having the time of his life. He saw himself as a successor of the intrepid heroes of Roman legend, sternly pushing forward to his goal against all obstacles. From time to time he was forced to resume his feeble attempts at paddling, but always found that he could not master the art and made more headway by wading upstream. Everything was soaking wet— baggage, provisions, weapons, bedding, and himself. At night it was impossible to light a fire to dry out his belongings because the renegade Chippewa had stolen his flint, so he slept in his sodden clothing and relied on the morning sunshine to warm his chilled body. To add to his discomfort, the weather was sultry and there were many thundershowers. Beltrami himself did not care—wading in the river, he could hardly have been wetter—but his baggage was drenched and began to grow moldy. Therefore on the third day of his extraordinary trek he unpacked the ultimate item in his gentleman-traveller kit—a large umbrella covered with red silk. This he unfolded and stuck upright in the canoe so that his luggage was sheltered from the rain. Then he plunged back into the water, took up the tow rope, and proceeded on his "promenade."

The progress of Beltrami and his red silk umbrella is the last flamboyant episode in the story of Mississippi exploration. There is something captivating about the idea of this lighthearted Italian coxcomb trudging purposefully up the riverbed, waist deep in water, towing his canoe behind him because he did not know how to paddle. The exact location of the Mississippi's source was no longer important to anyone except a cartographer or the most romantic dreamer. Yet Beltrami was utterly absorbed in his mission to find it. To him, the most remote feeder stream of the "Father of Waters" was a glittering prize, an exercise in adventure for a cultivated man.

Beltrami's labors were almost over. After one more lonely night on the bank, tormented by mosquitoes, he encountered at noon the following day two canoes of Indians paddling downstream. The natives were thrown into confusion by the sight of the half-submerged explorer. Beltrami, shouting and hallooing with relief, persuaded them to approach the extraordinary spectacle of the "great red skin" and the crazy white man walking in the water. The Indians, Chippewa from Red Lake, came forward nervously, and the Italian had to distribute odds and ends of cloth and food to all of them before they would take him seriously. After much haggling, Beltrami succeeded in enticing one of the Indians, an old man, to paddle him up to Red Lake. It was a pleasant change from wading, but the philosophical Italian still had some conclusions to draw from his adventures. "You have experienced," he told himself, "complete solitude, you have tasted genuine independence, you will from this time never enjoy them more. The independence and solitude represented in books, or to be found among civilized nations are vain and chimerical. And, later, "I at that moment fully comprehended why the Indians consider themselves happier than cultivated nations, and far superior to them."

On the journey to Red Lake, Beltrami was nearly abandoned a second time. His "patriarchal companion" was an accomplished canoeist and paddled the explorer upstream at a fast pace. Beltrami shot a brace of wild ducks for dinner, and after the meal settled down to sleep on the bank, taking the precaution of tying the bow line of the canoe to his ankle in case the Indian should attempt to steal his boat during the night. Awakened by something tugging at the rope, the Italian raised his musket and let fly into the darkness. With a loud yelp his elderly guide, who had been sleeping peacefully, leapt to his feet and scampered off into the forest. Realizing his mistake, Beltrami blundered about in the dark, firing his gun and shouting at the man to come back. This encouraged the Indian to believe that they had been attacked by Sioux and it was not until the next morning that he timidly emerged from cover. In

daylight they found the cause of the commotion—a scavenging wolf whose carcass lay a few yards away from where Beltrami had shot him.

This incident confirmed the old Chippewa's impression that he was dealing with a lunatic, and all that day he tried to exchange places with every Indian they met. But Beltrami did not relish another bout of haggling and urged his boatman to continue. Dusk saw them almost at the entrance to Red Lake, and as the guide wanted to paddle all night, Beltrami curled up in the bottom of the canoe to get some badly needed sleep. He awakened to find himself alone in the canoe, which had been concealed in the rushes. The guide had very sensibly returned downstream to rejoin his friends, leaving the Italian to the care of the nearest family of Chippewa. These arrived and led Beltrami to their hut, where he was immediately savaged by the household pet, a tame wolf that tore the visitors' last serviceable pair of pantaloons. Beltrami's stay with the Chippewa was not a success. He was eager to travel on toward the source of the Mississippi but had to wait while a half-breed guide was fetched from the other side of the lake. In the interval his hosts stole anything they could carry from his belongings and held a funeral party for a relative who had been killed by the Sioux. The funeral consisted of the family's yelling, eating, drinking, and dancing without intermission until Beltrami, heartily sick of the din, wished that he could leave before the Indians consumed all the provisions he had brought with him. The *Boisbrûlé,* as Beltrami called anyone of mixed blood, finally put in his appearance, and the Italian realized immediately that he was going to have trouble. The half-breed was intelligent and could read and write, but he was a shifty character and it took all Beltrami's bluster and wheedling to induce his new guide to lead him to his destination.

On the morning of the twenty-sixth, Beltrami, the half-breed, and an Indian porter set out. The Italian was highly excited; he felt that at last he was approaching the goal of his wanderings, "the sources of a river which are most in a right line with its mouth." The little band crossed Red Lake and headed up a small tributary river that flowed in from the south. On the other side of the gently rising ground that faced them, Beltrami was told, he would be entering the Mississippi drainage basin. There, he was confident, he would discover the most northerly source of the Mississippi. It was a moment of personal triumph for the traveller, and he made the most of it. He savored the scenery and compared himself with Aeneas wandering into the unknown.

At last, after a final portage, he came to the crest of the divide. There, cradled in the top of the low hill, lay a small, heart-shaped lake. It had no streams flowing in or out of it, but a few paces to the north a small spring issued from the boggy ground and flowed north to the Red River; on the south slope there was a second rivulet draining in the opposite direction to join the Mississippi. After dangling sounding lines in the lake, Beltrami concluded that the lake and the two streams were connected "through long subterraneous sinuosities." At one stroke he had found the sources of the Bloody and the Mississippi rivers!

Sitting down on the shores of the lake, which he promptly named Lake Julia after one of his heroines (a lady "not my wife but a lovely woman"), Beltrami pulled out his pen and began, "THESE SOURCES ARE THE ACTUAL SOURCES OF THE MISSISSIPPI! This lake therefore supplies the most southern sources of the Red, or, as I shall in future call it (by its truer name) Bloody river; and the most northern sources of the Mississippi—sources till now unknown of both. . . . Oh! What were the thoughts which passed through my mind at this most happy and brilliant moment of my life! The shades of Marco Polo, of Columbus, of Americus Vespucius, of the Cabots, of Verazini [Verrazano] . . . appeared present, and joyfully assisting at this high and solemn ceremony."

Beltrami was ecstatic. He had found the source, and before him the Mississippi was "but a timid Naiad, stealing cautiously through the rushes and briars which obstruct its progress. The famous Mississippi, whose course is said to be twelve hundred leagues, and which bears navies on its bosom, and steam-boats superior in size to frigates, is at its source merely a petty stream of crystalline water, concealing itself among reeds and wild rice, which seem to insult ever its humble birth."* Carried away by his success, the excited Italian hurried along the course of the infant stream, scattering new names like confetti on every pond the Mississippi crossed; the Countess was given

her own lake, and such names as Monteleone, Torrigiani, and Antonelli were firmly inked in on his map sketch.

The downstream journey became a march of triumph. Beltrami now regarded himself as the intrepid explorer who was returning to civilization to announce the success of his mission. True to his role as a gentleman-traveller, he was magnanimous in victory: he made a detour to view Leech Lake, the farthest point that Pike had reached; Beltrami acknowledged Pike as "a bold and enterprising man," but he would brook no rival for glory. He could hardly wait to get back to Fort St. Anthony to advertise his accomplishment. He chafed at every delay and urged his half-breed guide to go faster. But the half-breed refused to be rushed and led Beltrami southward via a succession of Chippewa encampments.

The Chippewa of the upper river were embroiled in one of their periodic squabbles. Weakened by disease and liquor, the tribe had lost its former power and was dependent on government handouts. The war leaders, nearly all of them inveterate alcoholics, were quarrelling over who should be chief. The reigning warrior, a lazy drunkard named Wide Mouth, was being challenged by an equally indolent usurper, Cloudy Weather. By the time Beltrami stumbled in on the dispute, Wide Mouth had craftily suggested that if Cloudy Weather wished to prove his prowess, he should lead a war party against the Sioux. Cloudy Weather was eager to be chief but he did not want to risk his neck in order to oust his rival. As a result, the two factions welcomed the Italian as an impartial arbitrator. Beltrami was thrilled; to his reputation as an explorer he now proposed to add the role of peacemaker. His first efforts were extremely sensible—he advised the quarrelling chiefs to take their problems to Major Taliaferro, the Indian agent, who would decide between them. This suited Cloudy Weather, who saw a convenient excuse to avoid leading the proposed war party, but Wide Mouth was disappointed. Summoning Beltrami to his hut, he tried to persuade the Italian to send Cloudy Weather off against the Sioux. Beltrami replied with a solemn lecture on the responsibilities of leadership and the public benefits of peace. It was no use; the noble savage was stone drunk.

Beltrami's negotiations finally collapsed when the tribe managed one night to get hold of several barrels of whiskey. A terrific orgy ensued. The men and their squaws, all of them roaring drunk, rushed about the encampment brandishing knives, clubs, and muskets. The baying of their savage dogs added to the general din, and Beltrami's half breed prudently hid himself. Poor Beltrami was terrified. He found a safe

---

* Subsequent surveys have established the actual source as Lake Itasca (or, ultimately, Elk Lake and lesser bodies of water emptying into Lake Itasca), some miles to the southwest of Beltrami's "source."

spot just outside the camp and stayed there. "Standing on a mound of earth with my cutlass in my girdle, my gun in my hand, and my sword half unsheathed at my side, I remained a spectator of this awful scene, watchful and motionless. I was often menaced, but never answered except by an expressive silence, which most unequivocally declared that I was ready to rush on the first who should dare to become my assailant." Once he had to venture into camp to rescue Cloudy Weather, who was drunkenly defending himself against two opponents with a piece of wood. With the help of the half-breed, who conveniently reappeared for a moment, Beltrami pushed the raving chief into his hut and sent in one of his own faction to protect him. Cloudy Weather promptly went berserk, seized a knife, and repeatedly stabbed his guard until he was pulled away. Next morning Beltrami counted the casualties of the previous evening's excitement —twenty-four wounded and two dead. Understandably, his half-breed had decided to defect, and no amount of pleading could persuade him to continue the trip. Beltrami was forced to employ Cloudy Weather as his guide to Fort St. Anthony, and left the rest of the tribe to sort out their own problems.

The explorer's homecoming was not as glamorous as Beltrami had hoped. Cloudy Weather, suffering from a monumental hang-over, proceeded slowly. He also stole Beltrami's cooking pot, reducing the Italian to eating from a tin cup. But the returning "promeneur" refused to be daunted. He set up his red umbrella as a flag of peace, shot a skunk and cut up its corpse to see what made the animal smell so strong (getting himself soaked with the animal's fluid in the process), and clutched the sides of the canoe as Cloudy Weather shot the rapids "with an intrepidity and dexterity truly surprising." Eventually they reached the fort, where Beltrami jauntily scrambled ashore, dressed for maximum effect in moccasins, clothes made from skins, and a homemade hat of bark. Colonel Snelling and his family greeted this bizarre figure kindly and listened patiently to his flowery account of his adventures. Then, on October third, Beltrami, complete with his jumble of Indian souvenirs, took passage by keelboat down to St. Louis and from there travelled to New Orleans, determined to write a book about his heroic Mississippi pilgrimage. With suitable embellishment the reports he had been writing for Countess Medici-Spada became his text.

Beltrami's book did not receive the acclaim he had anticipated. Two editions were printed, one in New Orleans and the other in London, and neither sold well. Few people took his discovery seriously. It was obvious that the Italian had approached the source from the wrong side of the watershed. He had merely ascended the Red Lake River, crossed the divide, and claimed the first southward-flowing stream as the head of the Mississippi. To make his disappointment more acute, Beltrami found that the public was no longer interested in the whereabouts of the source of the Mississippi anyway. The topic was stale, and after a few invitations to high-society parties in New Orleans and a handful of favorable notices in the popular newspapers, the luckless Italian was largely forgotten. Only the professional academics and the serious map makers read his book carefully, and of course they demolished his claims with biting sarcasm. In fact, the rest of his life was sad. Most of it was spent in exile from his beloved Italy. Ignored both as an explorer and as a writer, Beltrami survived until 1855.

It would have cheered him immeasurably if he could have known that eleven years later the Minnesota state legislature would honor him in a way that even Beltrami would have considered suitable. Grateful for his rapturous descriptions of Minnesota's natural beauties (and undeterred by his questionable geography), the legislature named part of the state after him. To this day, 2,500 square miles of upper Minnesota are called Beltrami County.

Travel and exploration are the subjects that particularly interest Timothy Severin, the young British historian who wrote this article. Beltrami's incredible saga is one chapter of his book, Explorers of the Mississippi, *to be published by Alfred A. Knopf in February, 1968. "The Passion of Hernando de Soto," which appeared in our April, 1967, issue, was based on another section of the same book.*

Pride of the Seas

Nineteenth-century American courage and resourcefulness
carried our merchant flag to the world's harbors and our nation
to world prominence. The proud affection of a sea-conscious
nation for its merchant fleet is reflected in our portfolio
of ships by artists of three continents. Our essay,
by C. Bradford Mitchell, former editor of
Steamboat Bill and information director
of the Merchant Marine Institute,
charts the curious historic twists
of public attitude and official
policy that have alternately
fostered and stunted our
merchant navy

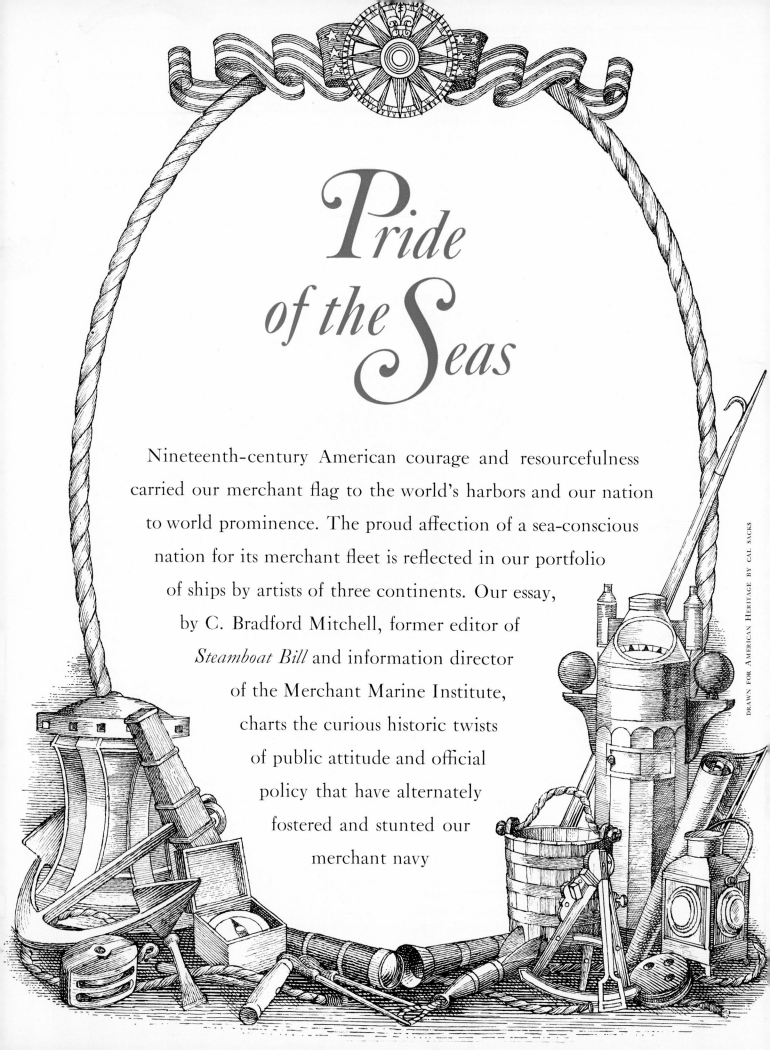

DRAWN FOR AMERICAN HERITAGE BY CAL SACKS

By C. BRADFORD MITCHELL

On February 6, 1783, nine weeks after the Revolution ended, a new flag flew in the Thames. It flew, said the London *Times*, from "the ship *Bedford*, Captain Mooers, belonging to the Massachusetts [sic]." That oil-laden Nantucket whaler was, the report continued, "the first vessel which displayed the thirteen rebellious stripes of America in any British port."

Such references to the thirteen-striped flag are commonly taken today as allusions to the red, white, and blue banner authorized by Congress in 1777. What is forgotten is that under Confederation the merchant marine of the United States had its own distinctive version of the national emblem, as does the British merchant fleet to this day. It was a starless flag of red and white stripes, symbolic, like the world's other merchant flags, of a maritime nation's pride in, and vast dependence upon, the ships that carry its commerce and bolster its wartime defense. After the Constitution was adopted, Congress never acted to confirm this American merchant flag. Since 1787, therefore, the Stars and Stripes have flown over merchantmen and men-of-war alike, a policy calculated to sharpen the focus of patriotic symbolism but, in long retrospect, prophetic of the submergence of identity and the ultimate decay of the "sister service."

When the *Bedford* lay at London there was no question what she and her kind meant to the young republic. American merchant ships and seamen had built the commercial prosperity without which the colonies could never have challenged the mother country. They had furnished the Continental cause what little regular naval power it possessed and, more important, a privateer force of dazzling speed and agility, which harried enemy shipping into the very harbor mouths of England. They were presently to embark on an exploitation of new and old trade routes which, despite Barbary piracy, depredations by both combatants in the Napoleonic Wars, and our own embargoes and nonintercourse acts, would win the United States an honored place among commercial powers and make the American merchant marine known from Copenhagen to Canton. Between 1789 and 1815, as the maritime historian Winthrop Marvin says, "it was dear to the whole country."

What broke up this love affair between Americans and their ships? Why, since the Civil War, has our average citizen or legislator been conscious of his merchant marine only in time of crisis, and unprotestingly allowed it to shrivel betweentimes? How does history's largest trading nation, with over 400 million long tons of exports and imports each year, come to have a merchant marine which stands fifth or sixth among the world's flags; which in terms of average age of its ships is one of the oldest afloat; and which carries only eight out of every hundred tons of our ocean commerce?

There are many answers, none satisfactory. Confederate cruisers are blamed for sinking much of the fleet and driving the rest to foreign flags. But Germany and Japan, almost obliterated at sea by 1945, were back among the ten leading maritime nations before 1960. It is said that we turned our backs on the sea to develop our hinterland (and indeed our patriotic song writers did veer from hymning Columbia, the gem of the ocean, in the nineteenth century to eulogizing amber waves of grain and alabaster cities in the twentieth). Yet Soviet Russia and Communist China, land powers with vast internal preoccupations, are efficiently expanding their merchant fleets while ours declines. It is also pointed out that the gap between American price and wage levels and those of foreign maritime nations has long since widened to the point where it cannot be bridged by any unassisted private shipping enterprise.

If the diagnosis is elusive, the symptoms are painfully apparent. Apart from the sorry statistics just mentioned, perhaps the main observation to be drawn from a thoughtful reading of our maritime past is that somewhere along the way we lost the knack, or the will, to follow through on our technical and commercial initiatives. At some point the native ingenuity and enterprise that had made us a leading seafaring nation were infected with a subtle infirmity of purpose. Thus we were able—with the *Savannah* in 1819—to give the world steam power at sea but were unable to grasp the benefits of that epoch-making innovation; able to perceive the cost of supplying our country's shipping needs but too irresolute to pay that cost. Looking back over the past 150 years, we can see this strangely uncharacteristic American trait at work misshaping our maritime destiny.

But it was not so in the beginning.

From earliest colonial times, much of the creativity and the exploitive energy of the Atlantic seaboard community was channelled into shipbuilding, navigation, and sea trading. Oceanworthy vessels were launched by both English and Dutch groups before 1620. A 400-ton ship—very big for the period—was built by 1645, and between 1674 and 1714 New England alone produced 1,332 vessels, 239 of them for sale abroad.

As American ships became known for their quality and cheapness (to the extent that by 1720 British builders

TEXT CONTINUED ON PAGE 81
PORTFOLIO OF ILLUSTRATIONS BEGINS OVERLEAF

The world's second commercially successful steam vessel, the Phoenix, *built in 1808 by John Stevens of Hoboken,*

New Jersey, was the first to venture into open ocean. The painting is attributed to Charles B. Lawrence.

The 1,500-ton packet ship Resolute *was built in 1857 for the New York–Liverpool service of the Patriotic Line. She was painted by Lai*

Sung, a celebrated ship portraitist, after she was later transferred to the China trade.

Boston artist John E. C. Peterson depicted the 1,400-ton Neptune *running through the Grand Banks fishing fleet in 1866. She was one of the*

last two packets built, in 1855, for the famous pioneer Black Ball Line, then in its thirty-ninth year.

This storm-tossed ship is probably the 1,961-ton clipper Young America, *which ran from New York to Cape Horn in forty-nine days in 1856*

and, two years later, sailed from Liverpool to Melbourne in seventy-one. The painting is by James E. Buttersworth.

The first American-flag steamship in regular transatlantic service, the 1,640-ton Washington *of the Ocean Steam Navigation Company, enters the busy port of Bremerhaven on her 1847 maiden voyage. The artist is unknown.*

COLLECTION OF FRANK O. BRAYNARD

This is
unbelievable?
What a picture!

Punch *called the 2,723-ton Collins liner* Baltic *the proudest "Yankee Doodle notion" of her day. In 1852, with a transatlantic dash of nin*

nd a half days, she became the last American winner of the "blue riband" for a century. The artist is unknown.

In June, 1857, the five-year-old coastwise paddler Black Warrior *established a record of four days, twelve hours from New York to Havana*

e 1,556-tonner, depicted entering Havana Harbor by J. Evans, was the pride of the Livingston Line.

This American Line poster depicts its liner St. Louis *in peacetime colors and as a Spanish-American War armed cruiser.*

were urging their government to limit the size of ships built in the colonies, and to bar them from all but British trade), they gained increasing fame for speed. The clipper ship was as yet undreamed of, but the Yankee obsession for "going at a good clip" was well developed—partly from the ever-present necessity of outrunning not only pirates and foreign privateers but, as often as not, His Majesty's own ships, trying to enforce the navigation and trade acts. Speeds of nine or ten knots on commercial voyages seem to have been routine by the 1760's, and it can hardly have surprised the British that, when war did come, these same merchantmen—oversparred and overcanvassed for the occasion—outpaced, outmaneuvered, and frequently outfought the king's heavier ships.

Survival in a world of restrictive trade legislation demanded of the colonial merchant and seafarer the utmost resourcefulness and ingenuity. Pre-Revolution fortunes, such as they were, resulted from shrewd assessment and intensive cultivation of the few permissible trades, combined with a liberal dash of privateering and no small amount of judicious lawbreaking.

The fund of commercial stratagem thus acquired was invaluable when the war's end brought political independence and potential economic ruin. Six months after the Peace of Paris, New York and New England shipping men acted to break the paralysis with which the merchant marine was threatened by the loss of English markets and the aggressive invasion of our transatlantic trade by the other maritime powers of Europe. Their daring departure was to open direct trade with the Far East, heretofore a British preserve.

Around the Cape of Good Hope to Canton went the diminutive *Empress of China* of New York, departing on Washington's Birthday, 1784. Close behind came the ex-privateer *Grand Turk* of Salem, already the first American ship to reach the Cape. In 1787 two small Boston ships, the 213-ton *Columbia* and the 90-ton *Lady Washington,* sailed together for the relatively unexplored northwest coast of our continent and successfully inaugurated a commercial cycle that put the China trade on a paying basis: trinkets and "trade goods" were exchanged with the coast Indians for sea-otter skins, to be traded at Canton for merchandise worth many times the value of the outward cargo. When she returned to Boston in 1790, having left the *Lady Washington* on the northwest coast, the *Columbia* became the first American ship to round Cape Horn and to circumnavigate the globe. On her second voyage, she discovered and named the Columbia River.

These and similar accomplishments in ship crea-

tion, ship operation, and mercantile expansion were "whole" achievements, in that they created something new and capitalized on it to the full. As a consequence, between 1789 and 1810 American-flag tonnage in overseas trade increased by seven hundred per cent, to nearly a million tons, and the portion of United States foreign commerce carried in United States-registered ships rose swiftly to the ninety per cent level, despite the extraordinary difficulties and perils then besetting any American ship on the high seas.

Columbia was now seriously challenging the claim of her dowager parent to be mistress of the seas. The thesis of this essay is that she could do so only because she had two sound maritime arms, a right which was brilliantly innovative, and a left which was belligerently executive. Her challenge, a major provocation of the War of 1812, would seem vindicated by the war's outcome; yet, only four years later came the episode of the *Savannah* and the first sign of that strange and costly withering of the important left arm.

But first it is necessary to note one more spectacular American invention, which was brilliantly followed up. On a snowy Monday, January 5, 1818, the *James Monroe,* a somewhat "sharp-built" but otherwise not unusual square-rigged ship of 424 tons, sailed from New York for Liverpool. She was the newest and largest in "a regular succession" of four ships between those ports, as announced by her New York proprietors. Their enterprise is known to history and balladry as the Black Ball Line, and it set the pattern of ship operation that has precedence in the American merchant marine to this day.

What distinguished the *James Monroe*—and made her voyage such a gamble for her owners—was that she had sailed at a scheduled time, announced over two months before. Moreover, she sailed with a cargo that filled only about three-fourths of her capacity, in a day when "full and down" was the first imperative, no matter how long a ship lay in port awaiting the last ton of cargo. Her passengers had been offered special inducements in the way of accommodation and sustenance, after centuries in which ocean travel had been an ordeal to be avoided. Finally, though her owners could not have known this as she passed Sandy Hook, Captain Watkinson would "drive" his ship to Liverpool in twenty-eight days, twelve days less than the time of most other ships then sailing the route.

These were the ingredients of the packet—or, as we would say, liner—service born that January 5: departure on schedule, "full or not full"; special attention to passengers and high-value "express" cargo; and unremitting drive for fast passages, with ships designed primarily for carrying payload and only secondarily for speed. The idea caught on, and its rapid adoption and

The James Monroe *(1818), first ship of the Black Ball Line*

refinement ushered in the palmiest half-century of American shipping. By 1822 there were four separate "lines" operating between New York and Liverpool, and additional lines from New York to Le Havre and from Boston and Philadelphia to Liverpool.

Within eight years, the American packet lines had virtually monopolized the first-class passenger and premium freight business of the North Atlantic. They were also making swift inroads into the European emigrant trade.

The ships grew larger, faster, and finer. The 600-ton mark was topped in 1826 by the Black Baller *Britannia,* the 800 in 1836 by the Swallowtail liner *Pennsylvania,* and the 1,000 in 1838 by the Dramatic liner *Roscius.* The latter, famous for fast passages, belonged to one of the giants of nineteenth-century shipping, Edward Knight Collins. This tonnage crescendo reached its peak in the 2,145-ton *Ocean Monarch* of 1856. Like her smaller, more famous contemporary, the *Dreadnought,* she was sometimes called a clipper packet, but the term is relative, not exact. Both were full-built ships, sharpened for speed as much as possible. From first to last, the packet was primarily a carrier; she was a speedster only to the best of her ability —and her master's. In the true clipper, these values were reversed.

The North Atlantic packet services were a classic case of a "Yankee notion" that was followed up, expanded, and refined into a tremendously profitable enterprise and a national institution. Simultaneously with their advent, the share of U.S. trade carried in our own ships climbed back from its postwar slump almost to the ninety per cent level of the century's opening years. They introduced, for the first time in the history of the sea, standards of regularity, reliability, and luxury that would be taken for granted after 1900.

Yet at the very start of this exultant half-century, America had already missed the boat—or rather, the steamship. It was a small and not very impressive vessel, true, and anything but a success commercially; but, though few people sensed the fact in 1819, the *Savannah* embodied an idea as brilliant as that of the men who launched the Black Ball, and more portentous. Moreover, it offered a once-only opportunity, in rejecting which this country lost both the credit and the benefits of exploiting steam power on the oceans —after having already outstripped the rest of the world in applying it to inland navigation.

The steamship as an idea had been advocated for at least thirty years. John Fitch, who ran a steamboat commercially on the Delaware River for several weeks in 1790, said ocean shipping would be the chief beneficiary of his invention. Robert Fulton, who voiced similar views, was working at the time of his death in 1815 on a steamboat for the czar of Russia. Whether she could have made the transatlantic crossing will never be known, for Fulton's heirs completed her as the Long Island Sound steamer *Connecticut.*

Meanwhile, it had fallen to Colonel John Stevens of Hoboken, whom Fulton had barely nosed out in the race to produce the first commercially viable steamboat, to be the first to send steam to sea. New York waters being closed to his new *Phoenix* by Fulton's monopoly, Stevens in 1809 sent her down the Jersey coast to the Delaware. Her master on this trip was a mariner from Connecticut named Moses Rogers.

Ten years later the same Captain Rogers dropped down the Savannah River bound for Europe in command of his own 320-ton ocean steamship, the *Savannah.* In the interval he had steadfastly preached steam on the high seas. At Savannah he finally found men willing to back him.

A New York-built full-rigged ship just over one hundred feet long in the hull, the *Savannah* was closely akin in design to the newly introduced Black Ball packets. Her uniqueness lay in her engine and boilers. Their 72 horsepower drove specially designed sidewheels, which could be dismantled and folded when not in use. A further innovation was her "bent smokestack," fitted with a slanted and swivelled top section to aim smoke and sparks clear of the sails.

When she left Savannah on May 22, 1819, a date now observed as National Maritime Day, the *Savannah* carried neither passengers nor cargo. No one would risk either life or property in such a craft. Yet her machinery worked smoothly and safely during the approximately one hundred hours, spread over twelve different days, which were all the steaming her fuel supply would permit. She dropped anchor at Liverpool twenty-nine days and four hours later, having run from Tybee Light at the mouth of the Savannah River to Cape Clear on the Irish coast in twenty-three days and twenty-one hours.

Recalling the *James Monroe*'s twenty-eight-day initial crossing and the entire Black Ball Line's first-year average of a little under twenty-five days, the *Savannah*'s running time over a course almost a thousand miles longer should have convinced America of the advantages of steam at sea. Her design and accomplishments were extravagantly praised in England, a nation not much given to praising anything American. She was visited and commended by the President of the United States, the king of Sweden, and the czar of Russia.

But she made no money, whereas the new sailing packets were making quite a bit, even during a minor financial panic. Americans in general scarcely noticed her, her owners could no longer afford her, and the *Savannah* became a coastwise sailing packet until her loss on Fire Island in November, 1821. Europe, however, and England especially, saw the possibilities. Of about twenty-five steamers that crossed the Atlantic in the next quarter century, virtually all were British-owned or built. And American ocean shipping headed swiftly and prosperously toward a dead end.

The speed and prosperity never seemed greater than in the fifteen years before the Civil War. American ships, both sail and (belatedly) steam, were sweeping all before them. Profits still mounted from the North Atlantic packet and immigrant services and the China trade. New prospects of premium freights and passage money had been opened by the California and Australia gold strikes and by the 1849 repeal of the Navigation Acts, which admitted our ships to London's hitherto closed trades with India and the Far East. All that seemed to be needed to reap these rich prospects was fast ships, large ships, and more of them.

During this decade and a half, maritime America embarked on two flamboyant and largely unrelated projects, the creation of the clipper ships and the building of a fleet to challenge Britain's North Atlantic steamship monopoly. Both got under way in the late forties, both succeeded hugely, and both lacked utterly any linkage with the future: the one because it had no future to link to, the other for want of vision and determination on the part of an already divided nation. By 1856 both undertakings—and our merchant marine itself—had collapsed in fact, if not in the consciousness of a frustrated people who would find it more comfortable to blame that collapse on a war still five years in the future.

But for the moment there was glory. The clipper ship was a miracle. She has been rightly called the greatest aesthetic achievement of the American genius, yet her beauty was created for essentially shortsighted purposes, and at its loveliest—in action—was founded on some of the most savagely inhuman hardships mankind has known. Paradoxically, even the men she maimed and killed seem to have shared the nation's fierce pride in her.

She was not created at any one time or place, or by any one man or group—though the names of great designers like John W. Griffiths and Samuel H. Pook or of great builders like Donald McKay and William H. Webb are inseparable from her legend. The word *clipper* defined no single rig or hull form. She was simply an end-product of America's historic quest for speed under sail, combining and refining the fleetest features evolved in two centuries of building and rigging smugglers, slavers, privateers, packets, and "Baltimore clippers."

The ultimate clipper was larger than any of these. Starting about 1845 with the *Houqua*, the *Rainbow*, and the *Sea Witch*, the tonnage of these sharp-built, lofty-sparred vessels increased from about 600 to the 1,500–2,500 range by the early fifties, with one breathtaking leap to 4,555 in McKay's monstrous *Great Republic*. Some 425 such ships were built between 1846 and 1855—120 in 1853 alone. Because of this, plus the construction of numerous large steamships, America's oceangoing tonnage, after hovering for forty years between 600,000 and 900,000, soared in this nine-year period to 2,348,000.

Clipper ship records, achieved by flawless design and the pitiless "driving" of masters like Josiah Cressy and Philip Dumaresq, still astound those acquainted with the best speeds that even twentieth-century man has attained on the sea. As early as 1849, the *Sea Witch* made New York from Hong Kong in seventy-four days and fourteen hours. The *Flying Cloud* and the *Andrew Jackson* shared honors for the eighty-nine-day record around the Horn to San Francisco. The *Witch of the Wave* flew from Calcutta to Boston in 1853 and the *Sweepstakes* from Bombay to New York in 1856 in eighty-one days each. And in 1854, an *annus mirabilis* of sailing records, the *Champion of the Seas* travelled 465 miles between noon and noon—more water than all but a small minority of commercial ships afloat in 1967 could traverse in the same time.

The Pacific Mail side-wheeler Great Republic (1867)

The Grace liner Santa Clara *(1913)*

But 1855 really ended this bright era. With almost sixty clippers still to be launched, the world already had little use for them. The market was glutted, and operators could no longer afford to throw away capacity for speed. The clipper, always an extravagant investment, could never again pay off its purchase price in one golden voyage, if at all. And Americans, with mounting concerns to the West and South, suddenly lost interest in one of the fanciest toys any people ever had to play with.

The clipper ship was going nowhere from the start —except, of course, to one of the brightest pages in the history of the sea. Perhaps this was enough. But the nagging question, unanswerable 110 years later, is where the American merchant marine might be today if half the genius, effort, and money the clipper absorbed had been channelled in the direction plainly indicated in 1819 by the *Savannah*'s crooked smokestack.

Ocean steam had not, however, been a completely dead issue. Also in that year the exposed New York–New Orleans route was successfully plied by the *Robert Fulton,* whose owners briefly contemplated sending her across the Atlantic. With the introduction of a practicable screw propeller, Boston shipowner R. B. Forbes in 1844 and 1845 fitted the device to three ships, one of which, the *Massachusetts,* made two undistinguished packet runs to Liverpool before going to the government for the Mexican War.

Meanwhile, since 1838 the British had introduced on the North Atlantic a score of steamships, including the subsidized Cunard fleet. Finally alarmed by this evident competitive threat, Congress early in 1845 authorized mail subsidies for American steamships.

Contracts were let to three companies: the Ocean Steam Navigation Company (the Bremen Line), the New York & Havre Steam Navigation Company, and the New York & Liverpool U.S. Mail Steamship Company (the Collins Line). The Bremen Line was first to get a ship in the water, its 1,640-ton man-of-war-built *Washington,* which sailed for Europe on June 1, 1847. She broke no records and was in fact soundly beaten by Cunard's seven-year-old *Britannia.* The Havre Line did not get under way until mid-1850.

But the Collins Line was to be the heart of the experiment, the focus of popular attention, and the first casualty of that vacillation and fumbling which have marred our merchant marine policy ever since. However, when its first ship, the 2,845-ton *Atlantic,* departed on April 27, 1850, the mood was one of high optimism. To the crowd that cheered her down the bay, Collins was a popular name, identified with record-breaking packet ships. Moreover, Collins was meeting Cunard on its own racecourse.

The *Atlantic* made good the challenge. On her first two voyages she twice lowered the westbound record, only to be beaten in September by her sister *Pacific.* Two years later the *Baltic* crossed in nine days and thirteen and a half hours and became the last American-flag liner to win the Atlantic "blue riband" for precisely one hundred years. *Punch* quipped that

> *. . . British agents, no way slow*
> *Her merits to discover,*
> *Have gone and bought her—just to tow*
> *The Cunard's packets over.*

Like the clippers, Collins' wooden side-wheelers were costly to build and costly to operate. Though they carried sails (and sometimes needed them, as when the *Atlantic* broke her shaft in mid-ocean and had to ride the wind back to England), they had an essentially "modern" look. They eschewed clipper bows and bowsprits; their straight stems and massive funnels spoke power as well as speed.

As record succeeded record and as passengers flocked to them, public enthusiasm reached a pitch almost equal to that generated by the extreme clippers. Speed and luxury—also the cardinal virtues of packet ships— came naturally to Collins, and, anyway, there was no question that they were what Congress and the public wanted for their money. So the steamers were driven as hard as the clippers, with high maintenance costs and low safety margins. Double catastrophe resulted.

On September 27, 1854, in a Grand Banks fog, the *Arctic* crashed almost head-on into the little French screw steamer *Vesta.* It was David and Goliath. The *Vesta*'s iron hull and watertight bulkheads kept her afloat; the *Arctic* sank with more than 300 people, including most of Collins' own family. Sixteen months later the *Pacific*, racing across the winter ocean to maintain her laurels against the new iron Cunarder *Persia*, disappeared with 186 on board. Since the *Persia* herself reported glancing off an iceberg, it seems clear that the *Pacific* met the same fate that later befell the *Titanic*.

Collins was broken, personally and financially. "Economy" and sectionalism in Congress killed the Atlantic mail subsidies, and the panic of 1857 removed any remote chance of the three lines' surviving without them. Most of the subsidized liners themselves rendered useful service to the Union cause. But not for almost four decades was another major American passenger ship built for Atlantic service.

The half-century from 1865 to 1915 was one of deepening eclipse for the merchant marine. When the Confederate cruisers struck their colors, the 2.5 million tons of 1861 had been reduced to 1.5 million. By 1900 this had been almost halved: 816,000 tons. The portion of U.S. trade carried in U.S. ships slumped from 65.2 per cent in 1861 to 27.7 per cent in 1865 to 9.3 per cent in 1900. Of course, these figures pertain to ships in foreign trade—the only ones with which this article is specifically concerned. Our coastal shipping in domestic trade, protected by law against foreign competition, *expanded* after 1861.

Unquestionably the foremost ocean shipping enterprise of this period under the American flag was the Pacific Mail Steamship Company. A product of the same body of mail-subsidy legislation that produced the Collins Line, it survived, in name, until 1925, becoming the longest-lived ocean carrier in our history.

Under the leadership of William H. Aspinwall, Pacific Mail contracted to carry the mails from California and Oregon to Panama, there connecting overland with ships of the similarly subsidized U.S. Mail Steamship Company, bound for New York. Its first vessel, the 1,000-ton paddler *California*, was en route from New York to the Pacific via the Straits of Magellan when news of the California gold discovery reached the East. Arriving at Panama on January 17, 1849, she found 726 forty-niners who had left New York weeks after her departure waiting to storm her 250 passenger accommodations!

With greatness thus thrust upon it by one of history's more improbable coincidences, the Pacific Mail, originally a precarious lifeline to the nation's recently acquired Pacific outposts, suddenly found itself a key instrument in the commercial growth of the far West. By 1867 it was ready to extend its services across the Pacific to Japan and China, a route for which it built the world's largest wooden side-wheelers: the *China*,

the *Great Republic*, the *Japan*, and the *America*. Though already as anachronistic as the clippers of the previous decade, these 4,000-tonners, with their distinctively American "walking beams" rocking majestically between rakish paddle boxes, established our flag on the Pacific in the very decades when it was being forgotten on the Atlantic.

Though Pacific Mail later fell on somewhat seamy times, becoming a financial pawn of rail interests and at one time the vortex of a subsidy scandal, it remained the foremost name in Pacific shipping until the First World War. It replaced its paddlers with the largest iron steamships yet built in this country, the *City of Peking* and the *City of Tokio*, and in 1903 and 1904 launched the 13,000-ton *Manchuria* and *Mongolia*, mammoths for their day, both of which long outlived the company itself.

By any standard, the Pacific Mail was a major shipping achievement. In contrast, our two most ambitious efforts in the Atlantic during the century's last three decades were characteristically barren of lasting results, although they produced a handful of proud ships.

Both bore the name American Line. The earlier, a Philadelphia–Liverpool line underwritten by the Pennsylvania Railroad Company, built four 3,000-ton iron steamships in 1871. The *Pennsylvania*, the first, took her maiden departure on the fifty-fourth anniversary of the *Savannah*'s sailing for the same destination. Though unsubsidized, these steamships managed to survive in the transatlantic passenger-and-cargo trade for a quarter-century, gaining a modest fame as the only regular liners under the American flag on that

The Panama Pacific liner Virginia *(1928)*

Standard World War I (foreground) and II freighters

ocean. But they were not profitable; the Pennsylvania built no successors and finally sold them to the International Navigation Company of Philadelphia.

This American company already owned the Belgian-flag Red Star Line and was about to acquire the British Inman Line. Though it kept the American Line fleet under U.S. registry, it ordered from England under the Inman name the 10,000-ton British-flag *City of New York* and *City of Paris,* the finest and fastest ships on the Atlantic when launched and the first twin-screw express liners.

Meanwhile, Congress had at last acknowledged the dismal condition of the merchant marine. New "postal aid" measures were passed, under the general terms of which the American owners of the new *Cities* obtained their admission to U.S. registry in 1892, on condition that two equivalent ships be ordered from American yards. The latter entered service in 1895 as the *St. Louis* and the *St. Paul,* 11,000-ton twin-stacked ships and the first truly first-class American-built tonnage on the North Atlantic since 1858. With the handsome three-funnelled *New York* and *Paris,* as the naturalized ships were renamed, these were commissioned as armed naval cruisers during the Spanish-American War—the *New York* and the *Paris* being temporarily renamed the *Harvard* and the *Yale*—before settling down to two decades of service on the Atlantic shuttle.

These new postal-aid measures were a plain instance of too little, too late. No resurgence of the merchant fleet followed in the wake of the *St. Louis* and the *St. Paul.* Rather, all the indicators continued their descent, and from 1900 through 1914, foreign ships carried over ninety per cent of American trade.

Since these opening years, the century has been marked by a few signs that the American public realized the gravity and importance of their merchant marine problem, and by serious, if sporadic, legislative attempts to revitalize the maritime establishment. But the overriding phenomena have been two world wars. To win them, heroic ship-construction efforts were expended, but these miracles simply left aggravated problems in their wake. The possibility of solutions has been made increasingly remote by the expanding

cost-of-living gap between this country and its maritime competitors, and by the emergence of labor as a powerful fourth factor in the already intricate industry-government-public equation. Above all, we have continued to demonstrate our by now historic indisposition to follow up maritime starts well made, and our boundless capacity to forget lessons learned.

The first lesson came when war broke out in Europe in 1914, and the United States found itself with practically no ships in foreign trade. The alien ships we had come to employ as our carriers (Robert Albion notes that in 1913 only 119 of 1,855 "departures foreign" from New York were made by U.S.-flag ships) had disappeared overnight. Our imports were cut off, and our export cargoes backed up in a stupendous traffic jam all the way to the Mississippi Valley. Desperate measures were called for, and for the first time in this century a shaken nation vowed never to neglect the merchant marine again.

By rifling the domestic fleet, building what we could, and admitting foreign-built ships to U.S. registry, we weathered the neutral years; but as actual belligerency approached, it was clear that a vast ship and shipyard building program was inevitable. We were, as in most other things, unprepared. Yet under the newly created United States Shipping Board and its construction arm, the Emergency Fleet Corporation, the yards were constructed (notably the huge one at Hog Island, below Philadelphia), labor and materials were obtained, and a total of 2,300 ships were delivered (mostly after Germany's unexpected collapse in 1918). It was history's largest shipbuilding program to date, and it cost more than three billion dollars.

The new fleet included about seven hundred large steel ships usable to make up our tonnage deficit; they were primarily of two standard cargo types, the 7,800-ton, square-lined "Hog Islander" and an 8,500-ton class bearing names starting with *West.* There were also twenty-six transports, a sturdy if unglamorous nucleus for our postwar passenger fleets on both oceans.

Also on hand when we entered the war were thirty seized German vessels, one of which was the mighty *Leviathan.* Originally built as the *Vaterland,* she became one of the best-loved ships (and still the largest) ever to fly the stars and stripes during two decades as troop transport and United States Lines flagship.

The Shipping Board's immediate postwar mission was to get all these ships into private hands or to operate them itself, as the nation's commercial interest might dictate. In doing this, it took a century-old leaf from the book of the Black Ball Line. By 1914, the cargo liner—a freighter operating "full or not full" on a fixed schedule over a fixed route—dominated world shipping. Now the board and Congress evolved the concept of "essential trade routes" and the principle that government tonnage be disposed of to private operators who would maintain liner service on specified essential routes for five years. By 1933, twenty-seven passenger ships and 218 freighters had been thus sold to twenty-one companies.

During this period—in 1916, 1920, and 1928—Congress enacted a series of comprehensive laws to stimulate, aid, and regulate the merchant marine. Despite past experience, it retained mail subsidies as the chief form of assistance offered, even adding a mileage formula that proved intricate, probably unreliable, and certainly unworkable. Senate realization of this led to the celebrated hearings held by future Supreme Court Justice Hugo Black in 1933 and 1934. While these disclosed few irregularities so serious as to warrant contract termination, they did bring the mail subsidies into disrepute, and Black's committee recommended scrapping the entire system.

The 1920 and 1928 acts also sought to avert the worst consequence of any crash shipbuilding program, "block obsolescence," by setting up construction loan funds to encourage replacement of ships before the entire war-built fleet wore out at once. While this fell far short of its objective, it did bring into being a series of two-stacked passenger liners, notably the *Manhattan* and the *Washington,* the first crack U.S.-built Atlantic liners since 1895; the *President Hoover* and the *President Coolidge,* America's largest Pacific liners; and the Panama Pacific triplets, the *California,* the *Pennsylvania,* and the *Virginia.*

The 1930's brought depression and, for the merchant marine, ominous signs of its customary slide toward public oblivion. But for once an alert administration and Congress countered the trend with what is still the century's landmark shipping law, the Merchant Marine Act of 1936. Dropping the euphemisms of mail pay and construction loans, they faced up to the fact that the chief burden for American shipowners and shipbuilders was the cost differential (chiefly wages) between operation and construction here and abroad. The act frankly provided for direct subsidy payments in the amount of this differential to owners and builders. Operating subsidy was also tied to the essential-trade-route concept, creating primarily another liner-assistance act. A Maritime Commission was created to administer the new arrangements.

The commission promptly entered into operating-subsidy contracts with a number of lines serving essential trade routes. Its architects developed a series of standard designs, notably the C1, C2, and C3 types, dry-cargo ships graduated in size up to 10,000 dead-weight tons. Operators were urged to begin renewing their fleets with these types. But before this program could get well under way, Europe was at war, and despite our neutrality acts, the United States was clearly headed for a shipping and shipbuilding crisis that would dwarf anything that had gone before.

Under its chairman, Emory S. Land, the Maritime Commission began expanding the nation's shipyard capacity, and had production well under way several months before Pearl Harbor. It was none too soon. The art of ship-slaughter by submarine reached its peak in 1942, and there were times that year when the collapse of the Allied supply system was avoided only by the infinitesimally widening margin between German sinkings and American launchings.

At first the emphasis was on the Liberty ship, a standardized 10,000-ton vessel propelled by already old-fashioned triple-expansion steam engines at ten knots, barely fast enough for convoy operation. More than 2,700 of these were built. Later came about 400 Victory ships, also an emergency type, but with turbines and speeds of sixteen knots. Some 700 fast 16,000-ton T2 tankers were of vital strategic value. Through it all, with a foresight unknown in earlier regimes, the Maritime Commission continued its "long-range" program and completed 540 C-type ships, the only ones that would be modern and sophisticated enough to meet postwar liner requirements. In all, just under 5,800 merchant ships were delivered, at a cost upwards of fifteen billion dollars.

With the largest merchant tonnage in our history, carrying seventy per cent or better of our foreign trade, we were perfectly poised for another long glide to block obsolescence—unless someone remembered. No one did, apparently, and for fifteen years American merchant ship construction stopped, apart from some tankers and a few superb passenger liners.

The United States *(1952), history's fastest passenger ship*

Steam and nuclear power, two historic moments in our maritime history, propel the Savannahs to an ocean meeting.

Among the latter was the *United States* of 1952, the largest American-built liner in history, and the first since Collins' *Baltic* to reclaim the transatlantic speed record, with a run of three days and ten and a half hours. She is still the flagship of the merchant marine, but her proposed sister has never been built, and in the space age her record seems secure.

As the active fleet shrank from 1,500 to 1,000 ships and the trade percentage in American ships fell to the levels of fifty years before, industry and government together worked out a plan of comprehensive liner replacement on the eve of the 1960's. This scheme was immediately slowed by the reluctance of successive administrations to budget funds sufficient to make up for the years of neglect. In almost a decade, about one-third of the liners requiring replacement have been replaced. Since these were only about one-third of the entire American-flag fleet, it follows that a great majority of that fleet is obsolescent today.

Faced with prospects darker than at any time in this century, the White House, Capitol Hill, maritime labor, and steamship management are agreed that a sweeping corrective program is needed. Unhappily, agreement stops at that point, even within the several groups. The trouble stems partly from policies which for fifty years have fostered liner shipping but have offered little real encouragement to bulk and tramp carriers or to domestic shipping (all but extinct since 1945). Be that as it may, the ironic picture in 1967 is of a worried administration willing to press for a positive new program but stymied by disagreement within the merchant marine itself as to the shape of that program. With this impasse, it is cold solace to possess about two hundred of the finest ships afloat and more twenty-knot freighters than the rest of the world in toto.

So, this essay into our maritime history, a history that has given us some of our most stirring accomplishments and no small part of the very foundations of American power and prosperity, ends, appropriately, with a question: Which part of that history will repeat itself? It seemed that we had come full circle when the administration announced early this year its intention of withdrawing the nuclear ship *Savannah*. Built, like her namesake, to demonstrate the efficacy and safety of a revolutionary new power source for ocean commerce, this beautiful passenger-cargo ship had indeed performed that initial mission in her five years of service. But, as with the first *Savannah*, there is more to do, unless the fruits of pioneering are to be turned over to others to enjoy and exploit. Germany is already building a nuclear ship; other countries are planning them. Our government's plan would have surrendered the initiative in commercial nuclear power application as surely as the scrapping of the first *Savannah*'s engine placed the initiative of the steam age in British hands.

But, amazingly, something happened which has not happened in Columbia's ocean world since that blunder of 1819. America rebelled. Shipping men, seamen, newspapermen, and a surprising number of plain citizens loudly protested the *Savannah*'s lay-up. And the government, heeding the protest, announced that she would be kept in service for at least another year. This of course does not assure her survival, or the continued nuclear primacy of the United States. But it has not happened before. Perhaps, for those who are too readily pessimistic, it is a hopeful straw in the sea wind.

For further reading: Seaports South of Sahara, *by Robert G. Albion (Appleton-Century-Crofts, Inc., 1959);* S. S. Savannah, the Elegant Steam Ship, *by Frank O. Braynard (University of Georgia Press, 1963);* Queens of the Western Ocean, *by Carl C. Cutler (U. S. Naval Institute, 1961);* Steam Conquers the Atlantic, *by David B. Tyler (B. Appleton-Century, 1939);* History of American Steam Navigation, *by John H. Morrison (Stephen Daye Press, 1958).*

failed, and he withdrew his followers from the center of town. The garrison, he decided, would have to be starved out. A heavy fire was poured at long range into the two buildings held by Hatfield and his men.

Two Marine reconnaissance planes, part of the nine-plane unit of World War I de Havillands based in a cow pasture outside Managua, happened to fly over Ocotal late that morning on a routine patrol. On glimpsing the battle below they streaked for their base. At three o'clock that afternoon a flight of five planes led by Major Ross E. Rowell swooped out of rainy skies and proceeded to demonstrate what air support could accomplish even in what the Marines called a "bamboo war." Major Rowell and his flight loosed small bombs and strafed Sandino's positions for a half hour before running out of ammunition.

At nightfall, Captain Hatfield was able to report that Ocotal's defenders had given Sandino a sharp setback. His own casualties included one Marine killed and two wounded and four members of the Guardia wounded, against reports from residents of the town that forty of Sandino's followers had been killed and an unknown number wounded.

Sandino, at any rate, was forced to lift the siege and pull back into the mountains to the east when a column of Marine reinforcements arrived. Several days later he issued a proclamation that he had attacked Ocotal to "prove that we prefer death to slavery" and added that "whoever believes we are downcast by the heavy casualties misjudges my army . . ." Another column of Marines and Guardia was sent into the mountainous heart of guerrilla country and occupied the village of Jícaro, which Sandino had renamed Sandino City and designated as his "capital."

The guerrillas had scattered in the mountains in what would become known as a classic pattern of dispersal following an engagement. At the time, however, the American authorities simply took the dispersal as a sign that they were giving up the fight. So convinced were the Americans that Sandino was beaten that they ordered a withdrawal of part of the provisional brigade to Guantánamo in Cuba and to other bases. General Logan Feland also left, after handing over command of the Nicaragua field force to Colonel Louis Mason Gulick. Meanwhile an Army general, Frank R. McCoy, arrived with orders from President Coolidge to supervise the coming election.

The countryside was fairly quiet that summer, and by the end of July there were only 1,700 Marines still stationed in Nicaragua. But the lull was deceptive.

Actually Sandino was quietly building up his forces for renewed and heavier fighting. A Marine Corps historian wrote later:

He was a master of propaganda and managed to use the Ocotal affair to his advantage: it served to attract the attention of communistic and other radical elements in Central America, Mexico and even in the United States; and it made Sandino a central figure to rally around. Considerable sums of money were raised, some even in the United States, and turned over to him for the purpose of providing military equipment and maintaining an armed force. Within a few months Sandino had several thousand followers and an actual armed force of almost a thousand. All this went on, however, without the knowledge of any responsible American official.

Harold Denny, the *New York Times*'s capable young man on the scene, agreed that Sandino may have become a hero abroad through "extravagantly false" propaganda, but in Denny's view "he did not represent public opinion in Nicaragua." His countrymen sympathized with Sandino but seldom offered their voluntary support. Many foreigners in Nicaragua, not including Americans, also sympathized with him because

he was an under dog making a terrific fight. I have heard foreigners in fear of an imminent attack on their plantations discuss him with something akin to admiration. But few people in Nicaragua were really interested in throwing the Americans out of the country, even though they might not love them. To the more intelligent persons of both parties, Sandino was a lively danger to Nicaragua's hard won opportunity for a just peace. Toward the last even some of his supporters outside the country urged him to cease fighting because his warfare, instead of driving the marines from the country, was insuring that they would remain.

The only American to wangle a personal interview with Sandino during the year of his most intense activity as a guerrilla chieftain was Carleton Beals, a correspondent for the *Nation*, one of the most eloquent of the defenders of Sandino's right to foment a rebellion against the American presence. Beals made a long and perilous journey through Honduras and across the northern border of Nicaragua, entering Sandino country through the back door. Through his well-advertised sympathies Beals was enabled to "make the proper connections in Mexico and Guatemala" and follow "the thread of Sandino's underground with the outside world," through El Salvador and then Honduras. While travelling that clandestine route, guided by Sandino sympathizers, Beals was shown a photograph of the town of Chinandega after it was bombed by U.S. planes, and in his report there are foreshadowings of Harrison Salisbury's dispatches from Vietnam. "An entire street laid in ruins and sprinkled with mangled bodies," Beals wrote; "the tumbled walls of the hospital, broken bodies of patients flung about.... Was it so long ago that we called the Germans Huns for destroying civilian populations without mercy?"

Beals's interview with Sandino demonstrated to Americans that he was no mere adventurer but a man of intensely idealistic convictions. Sandino attacked the Díaz government as an American puppet, blamed American financial interests for all the troubles visited upon his country, inveighed against Nicaragua's sale of its canal rights to the United States, and blamed the country's economic plight on eighteen years of American intervention. Only in relating his military successes, Beals thought, was Sandino "quite too flamboyant and boastful."

One myth exploded by Beals was the much repeated charge that Sandino was being equipped with Russian arms. Beals examined some of the rifles carried by the Sandinistas and found that they did indeed bear Russian markings. Investigation showed, however, that they had been manufactured in the United States for export to the Kerensky regime, which gave way to the Bolsheviks before the weapons could be employed against the Germans; subsequently they were sold as army surplus to Mexico, and were among the four boatloads of arms that Mexico sent to the Liberal revolutionaries just before the Nicaraguan revolution broke out. Beals was not impressed with their quality, observing that some of them "exploded in the hands of the users."

It was Marine air reconnaissance that finally tipped off the American authorities that a new Sandino build-up was in progress. The "squadron" in the Managua cow pasture had been reinforced with new Corsair fighter planes, forerunners of the Navy's World War II carrier planes, and they kept a close surveillance over the mountains of Nueva Segovia province where Sandino was presumed to be hiding. In mid-October it finally became apparent to the Marine headquarters in Managua that their field commanders were right: Sandino was about to stir up trouble again.

The Marine aviators flying over the mountains of Nueva Segovia observed much activity on the trails. In October a plane piloted by Lieutenant Earl A. Thomas, with Sergeant Frank E. Dowdell as his observer, crashed near Quilali in the heart of Sandino country. The pilot of another plane in the same flight saw the two men crash-land and escape from the wreckage. A patrol was sent out to rescue them but became engaged in a heavy fire fight with an estimated three hundred guerrillas; the patrol was forced to withdraw after three of its men were killed. Marine intelligence officers later learned that Thomas and Dowdell were killed by Sandinistas after they took refuge in a cave.

About that time the Marines managed, from aerial reconnaissance and other reports, to pinpoint the center of Sandino activity. It was a mile-high, heavily forested mountain named El Chipote—meaning in Spanish slang "back-handed slap"—in southeastern Nueva Segovia. The mountain was fifteen miles long and shaped like a battleship. On its prow Sandino had established a fortified camp scored with trenches and pitted with foxholes and machine-gun nests. The Coco River flowed down just to the south of the summit of El Chipote, the Jícaro through a valley on its western flank.

Rooting Sandino out of that stronghold became the Marines' immediate objective. On December 21, 1927, two columns set out on converging marches toward the fortified hogback of El Chipote. They were curiously undermanned, considering the fact that Marine intelligence credited Sandino with having close to a thousand men under his command. One column— one hundred fifty Marines, seven members of the Guardia, and a long pack train, commanded by Captain Richard Livingston—marched from Jinotega; another column, commanded by First Lieutenant Merton A. Richal and consisting of sixty Marines and constabulary, set out from Pueblo Nuevo. They were to meet at Quilali on the Jícaro River and join forces for the climb up El Chipote.

By the morning of December 30, both columns were within a few miles of Quilali. Suddenly Sandino's followers, awaiting their foes' slow and ponderous approach, sprang a double ambush. Less than a mile south of Quilali, as it proceeded along a narrow trail clinging to the flank of El Chipote, Captain Livingston's column was attacked by a large force of Sandinistas from concealed positions above the trail. The guerrillas rained down fire from automatic rifles and trench mortars. (The mortars, homemade, had been produced by Sandino's armory at the Butters mine a few miles up the Jícaro. They were fashioned from lengths of iron pipe, and the missiles they fired were rawhide pouches packed with scraps of iron, stones, and glass fragments; the pouches were tamped into the pipes with charges of dynamite.) Before the column could fight its way out of the trap, five Marines were killed and twenty-three others wounded, six of them, including Captain Livingston, seriously. Their pack train was scattered and most of their supplies lost. Livingston's second-in-command, Lieutenant Moses J. Gould, took over the job of leading the detachment to the village of Quilali through snipers' fire on both sides of the trail.

A short time later the other column was similarly surprised a few miles west of Quilali. It took that detachment two days to fight its way out of a succession of ambushes; Lieutenant Richal himself was seriously wounded and three other Marines were also hit before they reached Quilali. Lieutenant Bruce, the machine gunner who had fought so valiantly at Ocotal, now commanded Richal's Guardia detachment; he was killed in one of the running battles.

The remains of the two columns barricaded themselves in the score of stone-walled and tile-roofed houses of Quilali; between them they could muster less than two hundred men able to shoulder arms. Against them were an estimated seven hundred guerrillas who had obviously been trained to a pitch far above that of the usual Central American bush army. The village was under constant fire. Its defenders would be starved out unless relief arrived in a hurry.

Once again it was the fledgling Marine air power, represented by the two-seater Corsairs and obsolescent de Havillands under Major Rowell's command at Managua, that was called upon to balance the odds. Planes on constant reconnaissance over rebel territory spotted the fighting at Quilali. Lieutenant Gould, now in command of the combined ground force, strung messages on wires stretched between two poles, which the pilots picked off with grappling hooks. Among other things, Gould asked if his wounded could be evacuated.

A dashing and skillful pilot, Lieutenant Christian F. Schilt, volunteered to fly out from Managua, land at Quilali, and remove the wounded—or at least try to. Meanwhile Gould and his men hacked out a landing strip. The only possible place where Schilt could land his Corsair was on the three-hundred-foot stretch of the road that ran through the village. Houses on both sides of the road were demolished and cleared away. Then, with picks and shovels dropped by other planes, Gould and his men widened the strip to seventy feet. Lieutenant Schilt would have to land on and take

Sandino's proclamations and notes were stamped with this "seal" showing interventionists what to expect.

off from a rough patch of ground about the size of a football field.

Somehow Schilt managed to pull off the evacuation despite intense harassing fire from Sandino's men in the surrounding hills. Another Marine pilot circled overhead and poured machine-gun fire into Sandino's positions while Schilt made ten nerve-shredding landings in the besieged village, took out ten of the most seriously wounded, and brought in supplies and a relief officer; it was one of the greatest flying feats of all time. Schilt was awarded the Congressional Medal of Honor.

The Marine air unit continued to support the detachment at Quilali by dropping ammunition and supplies, and by strafing the enemy positions. Captain R. W. Peard, the officer flown in by Lieutenant Schilt, took over the command and moved it to the San Albino mine, a more suitable base for operations against Sandino's camp on the mountain towering over them. Two relief columns under Major Archibald Young also arrived, by truck and on foot. On January 14, 1928, Captain Peard led his command up the trails leading to the summit of El Chipote, supported by a flight of dive-bombing planes, and captured one of Sandino's outposts. The guerrillas' camp itself was repeatedly bombed and strafed. On January 26, Major Young's reinforcements joined them and the combined force attacked Sandino's headquarters—and found it empty.

The moment that news of the heavy fighting at the base of El Chipote was received at Washington, orders were given for a heavy reinforcement of the Marine units in Nicaragua. General Feland was restored to command there, and rifle battalions sailed once again from Guantánamo and other bases until there were 5,700 Marines on the scene. The build-up came at an embarrassing time for the United States. It was the eve of the Pan-American Congress at Havana, and many Latin-American nations were restive over the American intervention. The State Department defended the increase of troops in Nicaragua by declaring that Sandino's guerrillas were "regarded as ordinary bandits, not only by the Government of Nicaragua, but by both political parties in that country," and that American forces would stay only long enough to make certain that a free and fair election would be held. At the conference the delegates of Mexico and El Salvador tried to bring the Nicaraguan question to the floor but were outmaneuvered by the U.S. delegate, former Secretary of State Charles Evans Hughes.

Meanwhile, the Marines and their Guardia allies were launching intensive efforts to catch Sandino and stamp out his rebellion. The northern area, comprising Nueva Segovia province and the adjoining territory where Sandino's bands were operating, was declared a military zone and was handed over to Colonel Robert H. Dunlap and his 11th Marine Regiment to be pacified. His patrols moved throughout Sandino country, often supplied from the air by newly arrived Fokker transport planes. On February 27, 1928, a Marine patrol was ambushed in southern Nueva Segovia: five were killed and eight wounded before a relief column rescued them.

Several weeks later it appeared that Sandino was making a push toward Matagalpa and its coffee plantations. At the head of 150 mounted guerrillas, he occupied the large *finca* of Charles

American Marines captured this macabre Sandino ensign.

Potter, an Englishman, appropriated all the cash and supplies on the premises, enlisted a number of Potter's workers, and then amiably enough departed. Scores of refugees from the district fled to Matagalpa for protection, since it was guarded by a Marine outpost of forty-five men. Undoubtedly Sandino could have taken the town the night after he left Potter's plantation, though a battalion of Marines was being rushed there in commandeered automobiles. Instead, Sandino and his mounted force vanished in the direction of the northern mountains. Evidently he intended to employ hit-and-run tactics, in the style that would become classic when codified by Mao Tse-tung and Che Guevara. Sandino hoped to keep the country in a turmoil and prevent any American-supervised elections.

Gradually, however, the Americans succeeded in bringing most of the countryside under control, particularly in the north, where Sandino had been able to operate almost at will. Vigorous and constant patrol action, along with the systematic destruction of Sandino's supply caches, whittled down the guerrilla

leader's freedom of movement. Suddenly, however, there was an outbreak of banditry on the eastern coast of Nicaragua, which had been quiet all through Sandino's activity. In April, a bandit gang raided an American-owned mine, took $12,000 in cash, and kidnapped the manager.

To combat this new menace the Coco Patrol was established under Captain Merritt A. "Red Mike" Edson, who became renowned as a tactician in the jungle campaigns against the Japanese fifteen years later. The patrol, on foot and in boats, moved up and down the Coco River from the eastern lowlands to the uplands of the northwest, where it linked up with patrols from Colonel Dunlap's 11th Regiment. On several occasions Captain Edson's special force outwitted and outfought the bandits who tried to ambush it along the jungle trails. Edson developed the concept of the "fire team" to spring any traps laid for him. Specially trained, one unit of the team would build up a "base of fire" the moment the force ran into an ambush; then other elements would quickly move out to turn the enemy's flanks.

The link-up between the Coco Patrol and the 11th Regiment's patrols not only protected the mines that bandits had been raiding but reduced the guerrilla activity almost to zero. At least the country was quiet enough, by November of 1928, to hold the presidential election. An American electoral commission headed by General Frank R. McCoy and staffed by specially trained Marines supervised the voting. General Moncada, the candidate of the Liberals, won by a 20,000-vote majority over Adolfo Benard, the Conservatives' candidate. On November 5, two days after the election, *El Commercio,* the chief Liberal organ in the capital, proclaimed in its banner line: "The United States is Vindicated Before the World."

Not entirely, perhaps; but the United States did keep its promise to end the intervention as soon as it seemed feasible. The Marine contingent was gradually reduced as the Guardia was trained by American officers to take over the job of maintaining order. The 11th Marine Regiment, however, stayed at its posts in northern Nicaragua until March, 1931. The reason for its continued presence was the still intransigent Sandino. Even after the Liberal victory at the polls, he stayed in the hills and maintained his disloyal opposition. Financed from the outside, he had "begun to carry on radical propaganda in the interior," as Dana Gardner Munro has written, having veered leftward of both legal political parties.

Sandino stayed on the run until 1933, when a peace agreement was worked out by Dr. Sacasa, who had succeeded to the presidency. Several months later,

Sandino was engaged in disarmament talks at Managua with Sacasa and Anastasio Somoza, who was the commander of the Guardia at that time. While Sandino dined with Sacasa's family and a few other guests on the night of February 21, 1934, members of the Guardia, outraged by the leniency granted him under Sacasa's amnesty, and perhaps encouraged by the American minister, Arthur Bliss Lane, agreed that the time had come to kill Sandino. Group responsibility was assured by signing a pact that they called "The Death of Caesar." When Sacasa's congenial group dispersed at about ten o'clock, their automobiles were halted as they emerged from Sacasa's grounds and the Sandinistas among them were whisked off to the Managua airfield to be executed. Somoza himself was conveniently in another part of town and, to the disbelief of the Sandinistas, refused to interpose his authority. A machine gun was positioned, a signal was given, and the prisoners were gunned down. With the Sandinista leadership went the whole movement; its remnants were wiped out within weeks.

Somoza refused to punish those responsible for the assassination. And so the theme of violence, which runs through Nicaraguan political history with the wearying persistence of a Greek tragedy, was sustained. Soon after, Somoza forced Dr. Sacasa to resign, and himself assumed the presidency. Twenty-two years later, still the dictator-president, General Somoza in his turn was assassinated. He has been succeeded in the presidency by his two sons. Early in 1967, Nicaraguan politics again figured in the news, no doubt bemusing veterans of the Marine campaigns of forty years ago who had believed they were bringing the American brand of democracy to that country. Anastasio Somoza, Jr., the younger son, was elected as expected—but only after a flare-up of street fighting in the capital.

The rebellious spirit of Augusto Sandino was not summoned up in any of the news reports of the last election. But it lives on, not only in the mountains where he fought, but as an exemplar throughout the Southern Hemisphere. He was the first to defy the armed power of the Yankee Colossus, and to show that such defiance could be relatively successful if conducted on sound guerrilla principles. Furthermore, his revolution within a revolution, tiny in geographic scope, demonstrated to all who feel that the United States is too quick to intervene in the affairs of its southern neighbors that the American hegemony is maintained by force. The lessons of his rebellion continue to be studied, if not in the U.S. staff colleges, then in the bush camps of Colombia, Venezuela, and other disaffected areas where guerrillas still fight.

A free-lance historian and biographer, Richard O'Connor is the author of Ambrose Bierce, *published last spring, and co-author (with Dale Walker) of* The Lost Revolutionary: A Biography of John Reed, *which appeared in the fall.*

The author found Harold Denny's Dollars for Bullets *(Dial, 1929) especially useful in preparing this article;* Banana Gold, *by Carleton Beals (Lippincott, 1932), also makes good further reading. A recent addition to the literature on the subject, and perhaps the most complete, is* The Sandino Affair, *by Neill Macaulay (Quadrangle, 1967).*

Statement of Ownership, Management, and Circulation (Act of October 23, 1962; Section 4369, Title 39, United States Code)

1. Date of Filing: October 1, 1967
2. Title of Publication: AMERICAN HERITAGE
3. Frequency of Issue: Bi-Monthly
4. Location of known office of publication: 551 Fifth Ave., City, County, and State of New York, 10017.
5. Location of the headquarters or general business offices of the publishers: 551 Fifth Ave., N.Y., N.Y. 10017.
6. Names and addresses of publisher, editor, and managing editor: Publisher, Darby Perry, 551 Fifth Ave., N.Y., N.Y. 10017; Editor, Oliver O. Jensen, 551 Fifth Ave., N.Y., N.Y. 10017; Managing Editor, Robert L. Reynolds, 551 Fifth Ave., N.Y., N.Y. 10017.
7. Owner: American Heritage Publishing Co., Inc., 551 Fifth Ave., N.Y., N.Y. 10017. The names and addresses of stockholders owning or holding 1 percent or more of total amount of stock of American Heritage Publishing Co., Inc.: American Association for State and Local History, Nashville, Tenn.; The Society of American Historians, Inc., c/o Prof. Eric F. Goldman, Dept. of History, Princeton University, Princeton, N.J.; Charles Bruce Catton, Irwin Glusker, Oliver O. Jensen, Richard M. Ketchum, James Parton, individually and as Trustee under Declarations of Trust for James Parton III, for Dana Parton, for Nike Parton, and for Agnes L. Parton and a Child of the Grantor, Joseph J. Thorndike, all of 551 Fifth Ave., N.Y., N.Y.; Virginia L. Thorndike, 520 E. 77th St., N.Y., N.Y.; Gerald P. Rosen, 3307 N.E. 16th St., Fort Lauderdale, Fla.; Merrill, Lynch, Pierce, Fenner & Smith, Inc.,* 70 Pine St., N.Y., N.Y.; Alexander Hehmeyer, 575 Madison Ave., N.Y., N.Y.; Arnold H. Maremont, 168 N. Michigan Ave., Chicago, Ill.; Roger S. Phillips, P.O. Box 11, Rowayton, Conn.; Shearson, Hammill & Co.,* 14 Wall St., N.Y., N.Y.; E. J. Stackpole, 220 Telegraph Bldg., Harrisburg, Pa.; Barbara Joan Straus, c/o Irving Trust Co., 1 Wall St., N.Y., N.Y.; John Thorndike and Alan Thorndike, 11 Owenoke, Westport, Conn.; Evans & Co., Inc.,* 60 Wall St., N.Y., N.Y.; Clark Dodge & Co., Inc.,* 61 Wall Street, N.Y., N.Y.
8. Known bondholders, mortgagees, and other security holders owning or holding 1 percent or more of total amount of bonds, mortgages, or other securities: None.
9. Paragraphs 7 and 8 include, in cases where the stockholder or security holder appears upon the books of the company as trustee or in any other fiduciary relation, the name of the person or corporation for whom such trustee is acting; also the statements in the two paragraphs show the affiant's full knowledge and belief as to the circumstances and conditions under which stockholders and security holders who do not appear upon the books of the company as trustees hold stock and securities in a capacity other than that of a bona fide owner. Names and addresses of individuals who are stockholders of a corporation which itself is a stockholder or holder of bonds, mortgages, or other securities of the publishing corporation have been included in paragraphs 7 and 8 when the interests of such individuals are equivalent to 1 percent or more of the total amount of the stock or securities of the publishing corporation.

* Held for account of clients, no one of whom is believed to own or hold 1 percent or more of total amount of stock.

10. Extent and nature of circulation:

	Average No. Copies Each Issue During Preceding 12 Months	Single Issue Nearest to Filing Date
A. Total No. Copies Printed (Net Press Run)	333,700	355,000
B. Paid Circulation		
1. Sales through dealers and carriers, street vendors and counter sales	800	800
2. Mail Subscriptions	325,000	341,000
C. Total Paid Circulation	325,800	341,800
D. Free Distribution (including samples) by Mail, Carrier, or other means	3,200	3,200
E. Total Distribution (Sum of C and D)	329,000	345,000
F. Office Use, Left-over, Unaccounted, Spoiled after Printing	4,700	10,000
G. Total (Sum of E and F —should equal net press run shown in A)	333,700	355,000

I certify that the statements made by me above are correct and complete.

Darby Perry
Publisher

The Great Meddler CONTINUED FROM PAGE 33

of the A.S.P.C.A. and released to the newspapers the complete correspondence concerning the controversy.

Some years and several incidents later, Barnum embarrassed Bergh again when he announced that Salamander, the Fire Horse, would jump through fire as one of the main attractions of the Barnum, Bailey & Hutchinson show. Bergh rose to the bait and sent Superintendent T. W. Hartfield of the A.S.P.C.A. with five agents and twenty policemen to stop the act. Barnum entered the circus ring and gained the audience's sympathy with a clever speech, predicting that, if he were arrested, "I shall place a hoop of fire around Henry Bergh that will make him warmer than he has been in the past and probably than he will ever experience in the future!" The fire hoops were ignited. The impresario himself leaped through the hoops, followed by ten clowns and Salamander. Finally, Superintendent Hartfield himself passed through the fire unsinged. The flames were artificial, produced by a harmless chemical.

Respect and even affection developed between the two extraordinary characters after Bergh defended Barnum on an occasion in 1885 when the latter was attacked for using elephant goads. The showman began contributing to both the New York and Connecticut anticruelty societies and announced from his home in Bridgeport that he was "the Bergh of Bridgeport." In his will, Barnum bequeathed a thousand dollars to Bridgeport for the erection of a statue to Bergh. The memorial was unveiled October 1, 1897; it had water troughs on two levels and was topped by a statue of a horse. In March of 1964 an automobile crashed into the base, toppling the horse and damaging it beyond repair. But the rest of the monument still stands at Main Street and University Avenue.

As the years passed, the A.S.P.C.A. kept a vigilant eye on the market for worn-out horses; on the city dog pound, where strays were executed with revolting cruelty; on the treatment of draft animals along the Erie Canal; on the condition of the stump-tailed cows of Brooklyn and Long Island (the tails dropped off milkers that were diseased). The cows, which were fed on garbage and distillery slops, produced milk that was sold as "Pure Orange County Milk." In this instance, Bergh's concern for animals resulted also in a severe arraignment of the dairy business, with beneficial side effects upon sanitation and public health.

Bergh is also credited with devising derricks and slings for raising large animals that had fallen into excavations, and with the invention of the clay pigeon to save maimed birds from the guns of trap-shooters. He also put an ambulance wagon into service for New York's animals two years before Bellevue Hospital introduced the idea for humans.

Finances of the society were markedly improved by a timely bequest from a dying Frenchman, Louis Bonard, who, ironically, had made his fortune by trading with Indians for the furs of animals caught in steel traps. The Bonard will was hotly contested on the ground that Bonard was a Buddhist and believed in the transmigration of souls. Therefore, it was argued, decedent had given his property to the A.S.P.C.A. only with a view to his own protection in case he found after death that he had been absorbed into the body of an animal—a theory the court rejected. The money enabled the A.S.P.C.A. to expand its activities and move to its own building on the southeast corner of Fourth Avenue at Twenty-second Street. There was a drinking fountain at the door, a gilded horse over the portico, a stuffed Newfoundland dog in the vestibule, and a permanent display in the office of captured instruments of torture, many still smeared with the dried blood of the victims.

Bergh opposed vaccination and took on the medical profession in a sharp controversy over vivisection. But a bill of protest failed of passage in the state legislature, "both houses," as he expressed it sadly, "refusing to interfere with the torments of experimentation . . . inflicted . . . on mute defenseless creatures." Bergh's A.S.P.C.A., and indeed all humane groups taking a general approach to the field of animal protection, later left the subject of experimentation upon live animals to organizations that addressed themselves specifically to the issue.

In 1874, a case of flagrant brutality toward a child known as "Little Mary Ellen" aroused widespread interest and sympathy after the emaciated child, clothed in rags, appeared in court displaying a mass of scars caused by repeated beatings with a pair of shears. As a result, Bergh and his associates (independently of their animal work) launched the first organized movement for child protection in the United States through a body known then, and now, as the New York Society for the Prevention of Cruelty to Children.

Henry Bergh's power and prominence, his frequent entanglements with commercial interests, and his peculiar physical appearance—he was one of the odd-

BERGH'S LATEST.

IT EVEN MAKES THE ANIMALS LAUGH.

When Bergh suggested that animal owners be compelled to provide fire escapes for their charges, Puck *responded with the cartoon above. The* Daily Graphic *once wrapped him in a horse-blanket overcoat (left).*

est sights on Broadway—all served to keep him and the A.S.P.C.A. in the news. Because of his idiosyncratic temperament, his rueful countenance, and, to some among the press, the unreality of his objectives, cartoonists of the day frequently delineated him as a nineteenth-century Don Quixote, mounted upon a bony Rosinante. To his active antagonists, and to those who simply preferred to let well enough alone, Bergh became known as "the Great Meddler."

Numbered among his tormentors was the Eden Musée on West Twenty-third Street, New York's answer to Madame Tussaud's waxworks in London, which exhibited an effigy of the president of the A.S.P.C.A. under the title "Henry Bergh in Bangs." The New York *Sunday Mercury*, often responsive to the special interests of sporting gentlemen, castigated Bergh editorially as "An Ass That Should Have His Ears Cropped," while the comic newspaper *Wild Oats* indulged in hyperbolic ridicule: "Cockroaches . . . insist on sharing the best," the paper said. "Rats insist on having a chair at the table . . . goats put on airs . . . hogs grunt delightedly . . . [as] unlimited sway is given to the very humane Bergh."

Anecdotes had it that as a child Bergh had manifested a special sensitivity to the welfare of animals:

once he jumped off a pier near his father's shipyard, one story went, and nearly lost his life when he attempted to rush to the rescue of a dog that some older boys were about to drown. Other unsubstantiated items were that young Bergh once persuaded his parents to give up mousetraps and flypaper, and that he had cured an aged mouse of neuralgia with Mrs. Winslow's Soothing Syrup.

It was often asserted that Bergh was a vegetarian, which conceded him a theoretical consistency while neatly labelling him a crank. But it was not true: Bergh's philosophy made allowance for "necessary killing." At one time he tried to introduce horse meat as an article of diet. Characteristically, the move was attempted in the interest of the horse, a quick and merciful death being preferable to the fate that awaited the victims of the horse markets.

Bergh's courage was tested on many occasions. He received numerous anonymous letters, embellished with crude skulls and crossbones and scrawled with BEWARE's, advising him to leave town. One post card named the day and the hour when he would be assassinated. A drayman, arrested for overloading his horse, took a cut at Bergh with a piece of iron; fortunately he missed. Once Bergh pulled two large men

THE ONLY MOURNER.

EVERY DOG HAS HIS DAY

ALWAYS ROOM FOR ONE MORE

J.A.Wales

PUCK

Puck *maintained that Bergh's concern for animals was monomaniacal, as this cartoon suggests. It once said that he might do well to "retire, at his earliest convenience, to the nearest lunatic asylum, wherein he can receive proper treatment for his affliction." Nor did his activities escape the notice of Thomas Nast; the cartoon at the immediate right is a fine bit of* reductio ad absurdum. *Bergh's abiding interest in horses is reflected in the sketch at the far right.*

off a heavily laden coal wagon that a single horse was straining to drag through the snow. Always he was accused of choosing the wrong target. The "dairy-maids" thought he ought to confine his attentions to the butchers. The butchers favored vigorous action against cockfighting; while Kit Burns, the entrepreneur of the civilizing institution of dogfighting, warned: "Your society is doing a noble work, sir, yes, a magnificent work, but let me tell you, when it interferes in dogfighting, it digs its own grave."

The A.S.P.C.A. was also charged with bearing down on the poor while excusing the rich. But the truth was that Bergh had difficulty when he tried to call to account members of the business and social elite; the courts held, for example, that unless an officer of a corporation personally hit a horse on the head with a shovel or left it to die in the street he could not be held responsible.

Although Bergh was derided and defied, the annual reports of the A.S.P.C.A. demonstrated that humanitarian sentiments were taking hold. Humane societies were multiplying, and in some states (Colorado and Wisconsin are examples) animal-welfare activities were carried on by government agencies or bureaus. The press, on the whole, came to support Bergh, for the good work of the A.S.P.C.A. was self-evident. By the 1880's, the cartmen of New York were tipping their hats respectfully to President Bergh, and the Fulton Fish Market men, who had once spattered his clothing with chicken viscera and fish heads, were giving their old adversary a courteous salute.

New York City, always Bergh's special domain, came to regard indulgently and even affectionately the tall old gentleman with the kindly yet dyspeptic face and the courtly manners who, when he stopped a teamster for some offense and saw a crowd gathering, would deliver a little talk on Americanism and kindness. The speech became known as Bergh's curbstone address. It always included the appeal to free men to obey laws of their own making. And in all he did, he always had a further objective in view, which he wrote out in French just three years before he died: *Les hommes seront justes envers les hommes, quand ils seront charitables envers les animaux.*

Henry Bergh kept bachelor hall during his later years in a brownstone house at 429 Fifth Avenue, with two nephews in residence, with his clutter of curios, his *objets d'art,* and his many memories. His wife had been an invalid for years, confined in a home at Utica, New York, where she died in 1887. The Great Meddler died in his home during the Blizzard of Eighty-Eight, and was immediately ap-

SOCIETY FOR THE PREVENTION OF CRUELTY TO ANIMALS. PRES. BERGH

THE ORIGIN OF SPECIES

Th. Nast.

MR. BERGH TO THE RESCUE.

THE DEFRAUDED GORILLA. "That *Man* wants to claim my Pedigree. He says he is one of my Descendants."

Mr. BERGH. "Now, Mr. DARWIN, how could you insult him so?"

"A VETERINARY HEALTH COMMIS-SIONER."

plauded as a man who had carried on a unique work compassionately, if at times imperiously, and who had created a profound alteration in the moral climate of nineteenth-century America. Mr. Bennett's morning *Herald,* which had gotten so much mileage out of Bergh's foibles, eulogized him, and the New York *Citizen,* an old antagonist, announced that "the man who loved his fellow animal is mourned by his fellow man."

Recognition took many forms. Milwaukee, like Bridgeport, erected a monument. Columbia University became the seat of a Henry Bergh Foundation for the promotion of humane education. Elizabeth Chase Akers' poem *Two Saints* compared Bergh to Saint Francis of Assisi, and Barnum, while observing that "no man is perfect," saluted Bergh's work in behalf of the animal world.

It is a success story quite outside the rags-to-riches convention of the nineteenth century that Henry Bergh, born to affluence and leisure, achieved his fulfillment in the role of "mediator," as he himself once said, "for the upper and lower animals." Although there is a long and fascinating history in both Oriental and western cultures of men's ideas about their relations and obligations vis-à-vis the animal world, there is no evidence that Bergh was especially grounded in the speculative origins of humanitarian feeling. He was not a zoologist, anthropologist, theologian, or thinker absorbed in theoretical questions; he resembled, rather, the "righteous man" of Proverbs who "regardeth the life of his beast" because that was the simple way of the just and good man. Bergh's concern for animals in distress elevated his life above dilettantism and inspired an enduring movement toward a higher conception of humanity.

A more imposing monument than the one over Henry Bergh's grave is the flourishing network of anti-cruelty societies that exists today in North America, along with the many federated humane societies, the specialized auxiliaries such as animal-rescue leagues, shelters, defenders of wildlife, and placement services for homeless animals. They testify to the power of a man whose ideas gave kindness a new dimension.

Gerald Carson's name is familiar to AMERICAN HERITAGE *readers; he is one of our most frequent contributors. His most recent books are* The Social History of Bourbon (*Dodd, 1963*) *and* The Polite Americans (*Morrow, 1966*).

Among the primary sources for his study of Henry Bergh were Humane Society Leaders in America, *by Sydney H. Coleman (American Humane Association, 1924), and* Angel in Top Hat, *by Zulma Steele (Harper, 1942).*

Providence Rides a Storm CONTINUED FROM PAGE 17

Dorchester Heights, Lieutenant Isaac Bangs lay under an apple tree: "What I suffered this night, I shall ever bear in mind." But no one suffered at dawn. The British had not even tried to land on Dorchester.

The storm blew itself out at about eight the next morning, leaving behind a cerulean, translucent, windswept sky, but also leaving huge waves that made any amphibious landing still impossible. And, indeed, when the troops left Castle William, it was to return to the inner harbor. From bobbing small boats, the expeditionary force disembarked into town. Boston was again too well defended to be successfully attacked.

Homer would have been sure that some god had ridden with that storm. Washington, as we have seen, considered the storm "a remarkable interposition of Providence." His philosophy did not permit him to doubt that Providence had intervened "for some wise purpose.... But," so he continued, "as the [principal] design of the manoeuvre was to draw the enemy into an engagement under disadvantages, as a premeditated plan was laid for this purpose and seemed to be succeeding to my utmost wish, and as no men seemed better disposed to make the appeal than ours did upon that occasion, I can scarce forebear lamenting the disappointment."

Howe might have felt different had he known what Washington had planned, but, as he understood matters, he was grateful for the storm. He had ordered an assault on Dorchester not because he believed it wise militarily, but, as Washington had correctly foreseen, because he "thought the honor of the troops [was] concerned." Now he could blame everything on the weather, a force obviously beyond the army's control,

and one which had given the enemy time to make their position impregnable.

Although the great storm of March 5–6, 1776, gets little attention in the American historical saga, surely it was one of the most crucial events in the entire American Revolution. Had rain and wind and thunder not intervened, there would have been on Boston Neck such a battle as the Continental Army actually was to fight only once, at Fort Washington in upper Manhattan, where the entire American force that was engaged fell to the enemy. In all other battles, the patriots had access to escape routes through which, if they found they could not stand up to the trained European regulars, they could scuttle to safety. But the troops Washington had intended to land in Boston could never have regained their boats. They would have been trapped, forced either to annihilate the British or to face total defeat themselves.

In planning this assault, Washington assumed (it was long to be his fault as a strategist) a precision in the synchronization of his different attacking groups that was almost impossible to realize in actual combat. Yet it must be remembered that the British, any one of whose officers might have been considered demented for devising such a plan, had not the slightest inkling of what Washington intended. The surprise would have been complete, and the British would not have discovered the planned assault until they actually saw the patriot boats approaching. This would have been Washington's greatest hope: regular-army minds— British or any other—were not at their best when improvising reactions to what their training told them could never happen. Yet the odds would have been greatly against the American assault. The patriots would have had to cross a mile of open water into the mouths of British cannon. Had all succeeded in getting ashore, they would have been 4,000 against the 3,600 that Howe had left to garrison Boston. Only if the columns, driving toward different points, had

Castle Island, the site of Castle William, as it looked in 1789. The American flag, firmly proclaiming the island's nationality, appears in this drawing to be almost as large as the fortifications.

98

A Frightful Example

"Twenty years ago," said the passenger with the red ribbon in his button hole, "I knew that man whom you saw get off at the last station. He was a young man of rare promise, a college graduate, a man of brilliant intellect and shrewd mercantile ability. Life dawned before him in all the golden colors of fair promise. He had some money when he left college. He invested it in business and his business prospered. He married a beautiful young girl, who bore him three lovely children.... No one dreamed that the Poorhouse would ever be their home. But in an evil hour the young man yielded to the tempter. He began to drink beer. He liked it, and drank more. He drank it and encouraged others to drink. That was only fourteen years ago, and he was a prosperous wealthy man. Today where is he?" The clergyman in the front seat, solemnly: "A sot and a beggar." The red ribbon man, disconsolately: "Oh, no; he is a member of Congress, and owns a brewery worth $50,000." Sometimes it will happen that way.

From the *Missouri Historical Society Bulletin*, April, 1963

succeeded in joining up according to plan and then, together, had actually managed to break down the British barrier at the neck of the Boston peninsula, would the patriots have had any real numerical superiority. And, as was to be proved again and again in the next few years, raw Americans were no match in close combat for professional foes trained to the bayonet and accustomed to maneuvering under fire.

At Dorchester Heights, the situation would have been very different. The patriots had demonstrated at Bunker Hill how deadly they could be when they had protecting walls from which to fire on an exposed enemy. Since then they had become a better disciplined and officered force. At Bunker Hill they had been outnumbered, but at Dorchester the two sides would have been equal, at about 3,000 men each. Thus, the chances were excellent that even if the enemy had finally taken the heights, the British would have suffered many more casualties than their army could have afforded.

It thus seems reasonable to contend that the plan Washington drew up with his council of officers and hoped to put into effect should never have included an attack on Boston itself, but should simply have been limited to the fortification and subsequent defense of Dorchester Heights. The history books, indeed, indulgent to the conception of Washington's infallibility, have tended to make out that in placing cannon on Dorchester he had completed his total objective. Praising the move that sent the British scurrying out of Boston, writers have suppressed or played down Washington's further intention of trying to win the war then and there with a second engagement in which the odds would have been greatly against him.

To survey the situation as a whole, not only what actually happened but also what had been planned, is to recognize the tempest as a piece of marvelous good fortune. It prevented Washington's fool-hardy optimism from costing him anything; kept the cause from being grievously or perhaps fatally damaged as it might well have been. Did the genius of America ride in that storm, delaying action until her amateur commander in chief had time to become more proficient in the art of war?

This article by James Thomas Flexner is based on a chapter of his book, George Washington in the American Revolution, *to be published by Little, Brown early in 1968.*

could you be so sure that he would not whip you?"

"Mainly," Croswell replied, "because I planned to run away if he had attempted it."

It never seemed to occur to Croswell that he was a David taking on a number of political Goliaths. One reason may have been the illusion created by the preponderance of Federalists in Hudson. Among his prominent contributors was a young attorney, Thomas Grosvenor, who was the brother-in-law of Elisha Williams. Williams did more than merely threaten Charlie Holt when the *Bee* turned some of its venom in his direction. He caught the small, thin Holt, described as a "cripple" by a Columbia County antiquarian, and with several supporters nearby, thrashed him thoroughly.

Meanwhile, Croswell broadened his attacks on Jefferson with other choice tidbits from Callender's pen. He quoted the erstwhile Jeffersonian as declaring that "Mr. Jefferson has for years past while his wife was living and does now since she is dead, keep a woolly headed concubine by the name of Sally—that by her he had had several children, and that one by the name of Tom has since his father's election taken upon himself many airs of importance, and boasted his extraction from a President." To this, Croswell added another noxious tale: how Jefferson, before his marriage, attempted to seduce Mrs. John Walker, the wife of a close friend.

Other extremist Federalist papers were printing the same stories. Publicly, Jefferson always maintained a philosopher's stance toward the abuse he was getting. In 1803 he wrote to a European friend, "[It] is so difficult to draw a line of separation between the abuse and the wholesome use of the press, that as yet we have found it better to trust the public judgment, rather than the magistrate, with the discrimination between truth and falsehood." But his actions in 1803 belied that view. One reason may have been that two out of the three stories the Federalists were spreading were uncomfortably close to the truth. The slave concubine would seem to be sheer slander, but three years later Jefferson admitted privately that the Walker story was essentially accurate; and even his most benevolent biographers find it hard to explain away his relations with Callender.

By private letter and personal messenger, in his wonted style, Jefferson passed the word to his state leaders. "[The] press ought to be restored to its credibility if possible," he told Thomas McKean, the governor of Pennsylvania. "...I have therefore long thought that a few prosecutions of the most prominent offenders would have a wholesome effect...Not a general prosecution, for that would look like persecution: but a selected one." For the already infuriated Jeffersonians in states where Federalists were most impudent, this was what they had been waiting for. Joseph Dennie, the arch-Federalist editor of the Philadelphia *Port Folio,* was promptly charged with seditious libel against the state and the United States. In New York, the selected victim was Harry Croswell.

Several historians have wondered why this obscure editor was singled out rather than the prestigious William Coleman of the *Evening Post,* who had also reprinted Callender's anti-Jefferson blasts. But even a rudimentary sketch of New York politics in 1802 makes it easy to see why Croswell was Attorney General Ambrose Spencer's number-one choice. There is nothing like smiting the enemy when he has had the effrontery to invade one of your most powerful bastions. To underscore this fact, Spencer himself appeared to prosecute the case, with the local district attorney, Ebenezer Foote, serving merely as an assistant.

Spencer was an ex-Federalist who had "gone over" to the other party, and seeing this turncoat undoubtedly made Harry Croswell seethe when he was brought on a bench warrant before three local judges at the Court of General Sessions sitting at Claverack, then the Columbia County seat. The fiery young editor was indicted for libel on two counts, which were duly read to him. One was based on the fourth

The only Federalist supreme court justice hearing the Croswell case, James Kent was still a match for his colleagues.

issue of the *Wasp,* August 12, 1802, in which he had listed "a few 'squally' facts"—five executive acts by President Jefferson which, Croswell maintained, grossly violated the federal Constitution. The second and more serious charge was based on a paragraph that had appeared in the *Wasp* on September 9, 1802:

Holt says, the burden of the Federal song is, that Mr. Jefferson paid Callender for writing against the late administration. This is wholly false. The charge is explicitly this:—Jefferson paid Callender for calling Washington a traitor, a robber, and a perjurer—. For calling Adams, a hoary headed incendiary; and for most grossly slandering the private characters of men, who, he well knew were virtuous. These charges, not a democratic editor has yet dared, or ever will dare to meet in an open manly discussion.

Croswell was not deserted by his Federalist friends. Standing beside him at the bar were Elisha Williams, Jacob Rutsen Van Rensselaer, and William W. Van Ness. Williams was already established as a legal giant. Oliver Wendell Holmes, in *The Poet at the Breakfast-Table,* wrote that he once asked a distinguished New Yorker, "Who on the whole seems the most considerable person you ever met?" Quite to Holmes's bemusement, the man replied without hesitation, "Elisha Williams." Van Rensselaer was a vigorous descendant of the great patroon family that had once owned 62,000 acres of land on the east side of the Hudson River, including the entire town of Claverack. Van Ness at twenty-seven was considered the most brilliant young attorney in Columbia County. His folksy courtroom manner was typical of the younger Federalists' new style. He often interrupted

Chief justice of New York's supreme court, Morgan Lewis was also a signer of the Declaration of Independence.

his speeches to ask the foreman of the jury for a chew of tobacco.

The tone of the trial was set from the very first defense motion. Croswell's counsel demanded copies of the indictments before entering a plea. The Attorney General objected and was sustained by the all-Republican bench, and Croswell pleaded not guilty. (In his *Wasp* memoir Croswell says that the Jefferson-Callender passage, which was to become the heart of the case, had actually been written by Thomas Grosvenor, but he declined to implicate this young man and took his chances before the court. This required courage. A sojourn in a crude county jail was no laughing matter in 1803.) The defense then requested a postponement until the next session of the circuit court. They argued that on an issue as legally complex as the law of libel, a state supreme court justice should sit. The Attorney General objected; he was promptly upheld.

The defense now made a most significant motion—a request for postponement in order to bring from Virginia James Callender himself, who would testify to the truth of the libel. Attorney General Spencer sprang to his feet, quivering like a wire. Under no circumstances would he tolerate such a procedure. They were trying this case according to the law of New York state. The truth or falsehood of the libel was irrelevant! All he had to prove to the twelve good men and true in the jury box was the question of fact. Did Harry Croswell publish these libelous statements against the President of the United States?

Thus in the small country courtroom before three farmer justices of the peace, the political-legal giants of the Empire State drew historic—and ironic—battle lines. Here was the Jeffersonian attorney general, backed by Jeffersonian justices, vociferously upholding the Royalist doctrine that had been brought to bear against John Peter Zenger at his famous trial in 1735.

But the Zenger case is by no means the landmark in the history of press freedom that has sometimes been supposed. The German printer's acquittal on charges of seditious libel against Governor William Cosby changed very little. The jury had simply disregarded the judge's admonition to disregard the question of the truth of the alleged libel, and the law remained as it was. Subsequent cases in New York and other colonies made it clear that American legislators and most voters were ready to support freedom of the press only when the press printed what they approved.

Essentially, in fact, what colonial and post-Revolutionary liberals meant by freedom of the press was a press free from licensing and prior censorship. When the framers wrote in the First Amendment, "Congress shall make no law . . . abridging the freedom of speech, or of the press," the key word to them was "Congress." The reason Jefferson had considered the Sedition Act null was not because it had muzzled his party's press, but because he was convinced that Congress, under the Constitution, had no power to enact such legislation. Writing to Abigail Adams in 1804, Jefferson would declare, "While we deny that Congress have a right to control the freedom of the press, we have ever asserted the right of the States, and their exclusive right, to do so."

Thus the Jeffersonians were not as inconsistent as they seemed to be in their stand on Harry Croswell. They rooted their opinion in the common-law tradition of England, best summed up by the great commentator Sir William Blackstone:

The liberty of the press is indeed essential to the nature of a free state; but this consists in laying no previous restraints upon publications and not in freedom from censure for criminal matter when published. Every free man has an undoubted right to lay what sentiments he pleases before the public; to forbid this is to destroy the freedom of the press; but if he publishes what is improper, mischievous or illegal, he must take the consequences of his own temerity.

But legal principles, even legal traditions, while they may be revered by lawyers and utilized in emergencies like the one in which Ambrose Spencer found himself, are not so sacred to the man in the street, and Croswell's trial soon made it clear that the Jeffersonians were riding a tiger of their own creation. The moment Spencer declared that "the truth cannot be given in evidence," Elisha Williams unlimbered his heaviest rhetorical artillery. Hitherto, he pointed out, it had been the first article in Spencer's political creed that the people possessed the sovereignty and that governors and Presidents were their servants; and that whenever the people should write on their ballots, "Turn them out. Turn them out," those whom they had rejected must fall. But how could this power, this sovereignty, be correctly exercised, how could the people "pluck down the vicious demagogue and raise and support the virtuous patriot unless their variant conduct could be faithfully represented? And what

Philip Freneau, now remembered chiefly as a poet, was also an anti-Federalist editor who stirred Hamilton's wrath.

printer would dare to represent such conduct if the truth of the fact so represented could not shield him from destruction?"

Almost immediately Spencer began to backwater. He first agreed to postpone trial of the indictment based on the *Wasp's* claim that Jefferson had violated the Constitution. But he insisted on taking up the second indictment, the charge in regard to Callender, the next day.

Croswell's attorneys appeared in court the next evening and entered a formal affidavit stating that the Federalists intended and expected to prove the truth of the facts as stated in the *Wasp* in regard to Callender and President Jefferson. Like a shrewd fencer, the Attorney General returned an unexpected riposte. He wanted Croswell bound with $5,000 bail on each indictment "to keep the peace and be of good behavior." Croswell's attorneys exploded in a chorus of objections. Not only was such a demand illegal and a violation of Croswell's liberty as a free citizen of the United States—it was indirectly an attack upon the freedom of the press.

Elisha Williams and his confreres spent most of the next day debating this motion with Spencer. Again the political deficiencies of the Jeffersonian case were evident. Spencer, representative of the party that claimed to be the repository of the true spirit of the American Revolution, spent most of his time quoting cases out of English common law. The principal citation was a statute from the reign of Edward III which granted justices power to bind over "such as be not of good fame" to be of good behavior. Williams came back with a rain of English citations, including the still politically potent name of John Wilkes. When this erratic friend of the American Revolution had been arrested for libel in 1763 and the King's attorney attempted to have him bound, the Chief Justice of England dismissed the motion, "whereupon there was a loud huzzah in Westminster Hall."

The Attorney General rose with a rebuttal that the reporter for the *Balance* grudgingly admitted was, "with the exception of a few indecent expressions . . . one of Mr. Spencer's most ingenious speeches." But in spite of his ingenuity, Spencer's motion to bind Croswell was denied. The Republican judges could not bring themselves to gag Croswell quite so flagrantly.

Six months of legal jousting followed. The Croswell attorneys fought to get the entire case transferred to the circuit court, under a New York supreme court justice, and Spencer struggled to retain it in the lower court, where he would have a local Jeffersonian bench and jury. In the interim, however, the Federalists scored a resounding electoral victory in Hudson and duplicated it in five other Columbia County towns.

The legal battle reached a climax on June 14, 1803, when Spencer and the Croswell legal trio once more clashed at Claverack. After a long and acrimonious debate, Spencer gave way and agreed that both indictments could be tried before a supreme court justice on the next circuit through the county. It soon became evident that Spencer had a good reason for accommodating his opponents. Chief Justice Morgan Lewis appeared as the circuit judge. A thorough Jeffersonian, Lewis interrupted Croswell's lawyers as they once more attempted to request a delay in order to obtain evidence from James Callender in Virginia. Such evidence, Lewis declared, concerned the truth of the charge for which the defendant was indicted and in his opinion the law was "settled, that the truth could not be given in evidence to the jury as a justification."

Croswell's lawyers argued manfully against this prejudgment. They maintained that Croswell's case involved a public libel, which made the truth of vital consideration. On that ground, they requested a delay until a commission appointed by the court could examine Callender. (At this point in his career, Callender was on his way to becoming a hopeless drunkard, and Croswell's lawyers probably felt that he would be a sorry witness at best; hence the shift to a commission to examine him at a distance.)

Judge Lewis was unmoved by the Federalist eloquence. When the Attorney General rose to reply, the Chief Justice told him it was unnecessary. He said he was "astonished" at the application, and repeated his view that "the law is settled, that the truth of the matter published cannot be given in evidence." Then, suggesting the nervous state of the Jeffersonian position, his Honor hastened to add, "I very much regret that the law is not otherwise; but as I am to declare what the law is, I cannot on this ground put off the trial."

The outcome of the trial was easily predictable. The only thing that really mattered was the Chief Justice's charge to the jury, in which he instructed them that they had but one thing to decide: whether Harry Croswell did in fact publish the scurrilous statements in the *Wasp.* It was left to the court to weigh matters of truth or falsehood, and also of malice, in determining the sentence. The jury retired at "sunsetting" with nothing to debate. Nevertheless, they remained out the whole night, and not until eight o'clock the next morning did they come to the bar with a verdict of guilty.

Croswell's attorneys immediately moved for a new trial, arguing that Lewis had misdirected the jury, and reiterating that the truth should be given in evidence. The motion was granted and the case was carried over first to the November term of the New York supreme court, and finally to the January, 1804, term.

In the meantime, both sides regrouped for the climax of the battle. The Federalists sought out their chief intellect, Alexander Hamilton. As early as June 23, 1803, they had persuaded General Philip Schuyler, Hamilton's father-in-law, to write the brilliant former Secretary of the Treasury for help. (In a style that typified the primeval Federalist, the patrician Schuyler described the case as "a libel against that Jefferson, who disgraces not only the place he fills but produces immorality by his pernicious example.") There is some evidence that Hamilton advised Croswell's counsel before the circuit court trial. Now, with the proceedings at stage center, he agreed to appear in person, gratis.

Down in Virginia during the same months, fate put a dent in Croswell's cause. In the midst of a drunken spree his potential star witness, Callender, fell out of a boat to find a final resting place, as one writer put it, "in congenial mud" at the bottom of the James River. But he left behind him his published works, including letters Jefferson had written expressing his approval of *The Prospect Before Us,* so his dirty work was very much alive when the supreme court convened February 13, 1804, to hear the final round of *People v. Croswell.*

For Hamilton the case represented an opportunity for revenge against his great rival, who was riding high on the crest of political triumph. Some of it Jefferson owed to Hamilton, whose unwise attempt to dump John Adams as the Federalist candidate in 1800 had done much to hand Jefferson the election. Aaron Burr had in the same year destroyed Hamilton's political power base in New York, manipulating the votes of the Tammany Society to elect a Jeffersonian governor, George Clinton. Discredited with his own party, Hamilton had retreated to his law practice, where he had already established himself by his sheer brilliance as a thinker and speaker.

More than revenge may have stirred Hamilton in the Croswell case. This strange, often contradictory giant, who was considered by Talleyrand to be one of

Ambrose Spencer, Jeffersonian attorney general of New York, became one of the state's first political bosses.

The trial of John Peter Zenger in 1735 for seditious libel is more famous than Croswell's, yet its effect on freedom of the press was less. Zenger was defended cogently by Andrew Hamilton (no relation to Alexander), here addressing the bench.

the three greatest men of the age along with Napoleon and Pitt, had a deep, instinctive love of liberty which was never extinguished by his vision of a compact organic society, organized and run by a natural aristocracy at the top. Now free from the inhibitions and necessities of party intrigue, which had prompted him to approve the Sedition Act, he flung himself wholeheartedly into Croswell's defense.

He brought with him from New York an old friend and staunch Federalist, Richard Harrison, who had shared Hamilton's mind and heart since their days together as Washington's aides-de-camp. With these two lawyers of the first rank was young William Van Ness, to provide continuity from the earlier court battles.

The opposition, meanwhile, had made a notable change. On February 3, 1804, Attorney General Ambrose Spencer had been nominated to the supreme court, but he properly abstained from sitting on the case, and summoned one of his political followers, George Caines, as his associate before the bar. Spencer's abstention left a four-man court: Chief Justice Lewis, who had already proved himself a devout Jeffersonian; Brockholst Livingston, who, true to his family reputation, was of a similar political faith; a third Jeffersonian, Smith Thompson; and a lone Federalist, James Kent.

But in force of personality and weight of learning, Kent more than equalled the three Jeffersonian justices. "The American Blackstone," as he was later called for his *Commentaries on American Law,* the most influential legal volumes of the nineteenth century, had been converted to Federalism by listening to Alexander Hamilton's magnificent speeches in favor of the Constitution during the New York state ratifying convention in 1789, and by the still more cogent reasoning of the *Federalist Papers.* It was from a friendship with Hamilton begun in those days that he had acquired his conviction that the common-law tradition was essential to the nation's future. Not all lawyers agreed with this in 1804. In most states, the best legal minds were debating whether they should not scrap the common law and create a whole new code, as the French had done under Napoleon.

The problems—and the advantages—of the common law were all too evident in Croswell's case. All of the first day of the trial and most of the second were consumed by excursions far back into the mazes of English common law, with both sides endeavoring to show that the legal tradition of an earlier and supposedly purer age upheld their view of the central question: whether the truth could be admitted as evidence in a case of seditious libel. It was something of a stand-off; but it did clear away legal debris and effectively set the stage for Alexander Hamilton.

By now the hearing was absorbing the attention of both the judicial and legislative wings of New York's state government. According to Charles Holt's *Bee*, almost the entire state senate and assembly poured into the supreme court chambers to hear the climax of the debate. They were there for more than the excitement of seeing Hamilton in action. Already a legislator had submitted a bill that would permit the truth to be heard in libel cases. The British Parliament had passed a similar bill in 1792.

No exact record of Hamilton's speeches in the Croswell case exists, but New York papers reported them quite fully and Justice James Kent kept ample notes. Hamilton began by emphasizing the importance of the subject and went on to examine what he called "the two Great Points"—the truth as evidence, and the jury's right to examine Croswell's intent. He insisted he was not arguing for "the pestilential Doctrine of an unchecked Press." The best man on earth (Washington) had had his great character besmirched by such a press. No, he was contending for the right to publish "the truth, with good motives, though the censure light on government or individuals." Above all he wanted to see "the check" on the press deposited not in a permanent body of magistrates, but in an "occasionally and fluctuating Body, the jury." He pointed out that in the American system judges were not as independent from the executive and legislative branches as they were in England. All the more reason, therefore, to anchor freedom of the press in the right of trial by jury.

Hamilton ranged up and down English legal history and even dipped into Roman law and scriptural texts, to prove that the common law had always maintained these rights, until it was corrupted by the Star Chamber courts, which only proved his point—"a permanent body of men without the wholesome check of a jury grows absolute." Then he turned and indirectly defended the Sedition Act, which despite its repressive intent had been directed against slander which could be proved to be "false." He declared that he "gloried in" the fact that the United States had "by act" established this doctrine.

From here Hamilton soared into a long paean to the juror's duties and rights. What if this were a "capital case" and the jury decided that it did not agree with the court's interpretation of the law? Everyone knew that jurors were bound by their oaths, in such a case, to vote according to their convictions. Were he himself

a juror, Hamilton declared, he would "die on the rack" before he would "immolate his convictions on the altar of power."

Throughout the afternoon, Hamilton all but hypnotized his audience with his dazzling oratory. Kent noted that he was *"sublimely eloquent."* The court adjourned at 5 P.M., and the next morning Hamilton took up the argument again. Once more he worked his way through an impressive number of citations to bolster his argument, but he soon got to the political meat in his morning's work, a digression that Judge Kent in his notes called *"impassioned & most eloquent,"* on the danger to American liberty, not from provisional armies but from *"dependent* Judges, from *selected* Juries, from *stifling* the Press & the voices of leaders & Patriots."

"We ought to resist, resist, resist, till we hurl the Demagogues & Tyrants from their imaginary Thrones," he cried. Never was there a libel case where the question of truth was more important. "It ought to be distinctly known," he thundered, "whether Mr. Jefferson be guilty or not of so foul an act as the one charged." This catapulted him into a eulogy of the dead Washington that in Kent's opinion was "never surpassed—never equalled."

Finally, he paid sarcastic tribute to the "other party" and especially to their "strange & unexpected compliments on the *Freedom* of the English nation." But, he reiterated, a country is free only where the people have a representation in the government, and where they have a trial by jury. If America abandoned the principles of the common law, a faction in power could construe the Constitution to make "any political Tenet or any Indiscretion a Crime." Sacrificing and crushing individuals "by the perverted Forms & mask of law" was the "most dangerous & destructive Tyranny."

As the stocky figure of the man whom Talleyrand said had "made the fortune of his country" bowed before the black-robed justices and retired to his seat, James Kent jotted a final note—"I never heard him so great." Thus inspired, Kent wrote a masterful opinion decreeing a new trial for Croswell. The power of his personality and his reasoning persuaded his fellow associate justices, Livingston and Thompson, to abandon their Jeffersonian principles and agree with him —at first. But Chief Justice Lewis, by now running hard for Governor, wrote a contrary opinion of his own. He also paid Justice Livingston a little visit, whereupon Livingston suddenly changed his mind. The court thus divided two and two, and the motion for a new trial was denied.

The prosecution could have moved immediately for

a judgment against Croswell, but no such motion was made. The Jeffersonians were already badly clawed by their ride on this legal tiger, and they had no penchant for further gouges. Moreover, the New York senators and assemblymen, having heard Hamilton's eloquence, had set to work on a truth-in-libel bill that was certain to pass; the Chief Justice was upholding a legal principle that was about to be officially invalidated. So the case was simply dropped. Its impact, however, was important: other states would soon follow New York's lead, transforming Harry Croswell's case from a *cause célèbre* into one of the bulwarks of our free press.

Croswell's personal troubles were not yet over. Ambrose Spencer returned to Hudson and brought a new suit against Croswell and his mentor, Sampson, for libel. Sampson settled out of court, but the stubborn Croswell refused to back away from the scathing comments he had made about both Spencer and his henchman, District Attorney Ebenezer Foote, in the farewell issue of the *Wasp*, which had appeared on January 26, 1803. Foote submitted a suit of his own. Spencer recovered $126 in damages; poor Foote, attempting to prove he was not a swindler and a blockhead, was ambushed by a host of witnesses who solemnly vowed they had seen him cheat at cards, among other things. The jury awarded him damages of six cents. This final act of low comedy was gleefully reported in the *Balance*.

Croswell now became senior editor of the *Balance*

Hamilton's success at the Croswell trial may have prompted him to raise his political reputation further by accepting Aaron Burr's challenge to duel. It was a fatal mistake.

and continued to do battle in the Federalist cause in Hudson until 1809, when he transferred his paper to Albany. This was a mistake. The Federalists there were in disarray, and his support was meager. Debts piled up; in 1811 a leading Federalist who had loaned him money obtained a judgment against him, and the harassed editor served a short sentence in a debtor's prison. It was one indication of the fatal deficiencies of the Federalists as a party. The "best people" were too interested in lining their own purses to make the sacrifices that a successful political machine demanded.

Totally disgusted, Croswell quit newspapering, took Episcopal orders, and after serving briefly as rector of Christ Church in Hudson, moved to Trinity Church in New Haven. He remained in this post, respected and eventually revered, for the next forty-three years. But he never attended another political meeting, or even exercised his rights as a voter. "His revulsion from Federalism was so entire," said one of his acquaintances after his death, "that in later life his tacit sympathy was evidently with the Democratic party."

Thus exit Harry Croswell. As for Alexander Hamilton, the sequel of the Croswell case was tragedy. During the hearings he had stayed at a friend's house near Albany, and in an evening's conversation, he delivered some scathing denunciations of Vice President Aaron Burr, who was soon to run against Chief Justice Lewis for the governorship of New York. In the course of the election campaign, the friend unwisely quoted Hamilton in a letter that got into the newspapers. Lewis won, finishing Burr politically in New York, and the embittered Vice President challenged Hamilton to a duel. The acclaim he won at Croswell's trial may well have played a part in persuading Hamilton to accept—in spite of his personal detestation of duelling, which had been redoubled by the death of his son Philip in a politically inspired duel two years before. Having regained not a little of the stature he had lost within his party, Hamilton may have been more inclined to risk the morning visit to Weehawken in the hope that it would be another step toward undoing his great rival in the White House, Jefferson. He guessed wrong, and paid for it with his life.

Primary materials such as court records and files of early newspapers were Mr. Fleming's principal sources for this article. Recommended for further reading: Legacy of Suppression: Freedom of Speech and Press in Early American History, *by Leonard W. Levy (Harvard University Press, 1960);* The Presidents and the Press, *by James E. Pollard (Macmillan, 1947).*

When Christmas Was Banned in Boston

Many a book, a magazine, a play, a movie, has been banned in Boston. But Christmas?

Yes, Virginia, Christmas was banned in Boston. On May 11, 1659, the legislature of the Massachusetts Bay Colony enacted the following: "For preventing disorders arising in severall places within this jurisdiceon, by reason of some still observing such ffestivalls as were superstitiously kept in other countrys, to the great dishonnor of God & offence of others, it is therefore ordered . . . that whosoever shall be found observing any such day as Christmas or the like, either by forbearing of labour, feasting, or any other way, upon any such account as aforesaid, every such person so offending shall pay for every such offence five shillings, as a fine to the county."

This decree was passed more than a generation after the landing of the Pilgrims, but it was merely a legal expression of the attitude they brought with them on the *Mayflower*. William Bradford's *History of Plymouth Plantation* records that in 1621, shortly after the arrival of a new contingent of colonists, "One the day called Chrismasday, the Govr caled them out to worke, (as was used,) but the most of this new-company excused them selves and said it wente against their consciences to work on that day. So the Govr tould them that if they made it mater of conscience, he would spare them till they were better informed. . . . [Later] he found them in the streete at play, openly; some pitching the barr and some at stoole-ball, and shuch like sports. So he went to them, and tooke away their implements, and tould them that was against his conscience, that they should play and others worke. If they made the keeping of it mater of devotion, let them kepe their houses, but ther should be no gameing or revelling in the streets.

Since which time nothing hath been attempted that way, at least openly."

The cheerless law of 1659 remained on the books for twenty-two years. When it was repealed in 1681, it was less a victory for the spirit of Christmas than for the king of England: Charles II and his royal commissioners were determined to make the colony's laws conform with England's.

Though no longer illegal, Christmas was still far from popular with the Puritans. Their dim view of what they regarded as pagan revelry or, alternatively, papist idolatry, was so pervasive that over a hundred years later Christmas in New England was a dull affair compared to the festive holiday of New York and points south. Edward Everett Hale, author of the famous novel *The Man Without a Country,* remarked in 1889: "When I was a school-boy I always went to school on Christmas Day, and I think all the other boys in town did. As we went home, and passed King's Chapel on Adam and Eve's Day, which is the 24th, we would see the men carrying hemlock for the decorations. But that was the only public indication that any holiday was approaching."

King's Chapel was Boston's first Episcopal church, where Christmas services were held annually from the time of its construction near the end of the seventeenth century. The services undoubtedly were very dignified, yet the Christmas greens, the music, and the lighted candles had a holiday appeal, and some of Boston's young Puritans were led astray. With a mixture of consternation and pride, Judge Samuel Sewall noted in his diary on Christmas day, 1697, "Joseph [his son] tells me that though most of the Boys went to the Church, yet he went not."

By 1711, things were getting quite out of hand, at least by the standards of such Puritan divines as Cotton Mather. "I hear of a Number of young People of both Sexes," he wrote that year, "belonging, many of them, to my Flock, who have had on the Christmasnight, this last Week, a Frolick, a revelling Feast, and Ball, which discovers their Corruption, and has a Tendency to corrupt them yett more."

Corruption or no, the celebration of Christmas made steady headway in New England. In the nineteenth century, repeated publication of such instant favorites as Washington Irving's account of Christmas at Bracebridge Hall, Charles Dickens' *A Christmas Carol,* and Clement Moore's "A Visit from Saint Nicholas" added fuel to the yule log, and in 1856, Henry Wadsworth Longfellow could write: "We are in a transition state about Christmas here in New England. The old Puritan feeling prevents it from being a cheerful hearty holiday; though every year makes it more so." That same year, the Massachusetts legislature finally gave in and made Christmas a legal holiday.

Today, of course, Christmas in Boston is like Christmas in any other American city. There are Christmas services in the churches, lighted Christmas trees in nearly every home, groups of carollers going about neighborhood streets singing lustily, if a little off key—and jostling crowds of desperate Christmas shoppers elbowing each other into a mood to make some wonder if the Puritans may not have had something, after all.

By DANA P. MARRIOTT

107

he had any more self-restraint" at a White House dinner "than he would have shown at a church supper in Uvalde, Texas." Later the Vice President pawed and grabbed the King. Then, according to Ickes, Garner "reach[ed] his arm behind [the King's] back as if in a semi-embrace. I suppose that . . . to Garner the King was simply a visiting Elk."

After dinner the President proposed a toast to the Anglo-American example of mutual trust and absence of fear, expressing the wish that "these methods of peace, divorced from aggression, could only be universally followed." The King toasted in a similar vein.

Guests then adjourned to the East Room for an entertainment chosen by Mrs. Roosevelt. It presented a variety of American music from Negro spirituals to popular tunes. Kate Smith forced a rearrangement of the program, fearing that she might be late for her radio show. Mrs. Roosevelt introduced her as "one of our greatest singers," whereupon she sang "When the Moon Comes Over the Mountain" and received polite applause. Ickes thought that Kate Smith "was awful, both in appearance and performance." North Carolina's Soco Gap Square Dancers stomped, clapped, and whirled through "Dive and Shoot the Owl" and "London Bridge." This perked up Garner sufficiently to remark that the Queen might have dozed off "if those fellers hadn't been raisin' the roof." The Vice President kept alert even while the Coon Creek Girls from Pinchem-Tight Hollow, Kentucky, strummed several folk songs. Perhaps the snake rattle in the leader's fiddle fascinated Cactus Jack; it made little difference to the rest of the fatigued audience. For nearly everyone the highlight of the evening was Marian Anderson, who sang "My Soul's Been Anchored in the Lord," "Tramping," and "Ave Maria." Garner, however, was unresponsive: "So far as I could observe," wrote Ickes, "he never gave her a hand."

The affair finally broke up at about midnight, and the King and Queen went to bed in order to be fresh for Friday's ordeal of meeting congressmen at the Capitol.

A number of congressmen had continued to voice their suspicions about the royal visit. Some thought that Roosevelt was trying to influence voting on the Bloom Bill, which would grant broader powers to the President and topple existing neutrality legislation by extending cash-and-carry provisions to arms and ammunition. The King's speech at Banff, Hull's frank talk with reporters at Niagara Falls, and Roosevelt's statement that he would discuss foreign affairs with the King although the "conversations would not

be significant" had not eased congressional doubts. The previous March, Roosevelt had confided to Senator Tom Connally of Texas that the King and Queen would be "coming over" and that he would "like to have the arms embargo repealed before their arrival." Unfortunately, the Congress had not moved that fast. Perhaps, the more wary individuals speculated, meeting the King and Queen under the Capitol rotunda was a devious Roosevelt plan to sway congressional sentiment. But most of the skeptical forgot these notions when the King and Queen entered.

Tired of Garner's antics in the rotunda, several senators shushed the Vice President into respectability when they glimpsed the monarchs. Senator William E. Borah of Idaho, a leading isolationist, stood at the head of the line to shake hands with a king whose country owed more than five billion dollars in war debts. This seemed unimportant to Borah now. He had even taken out of mothballs a morning suit which he had not worn in thirty-five years, to look his best for the King.

George VI and Elizabeth, as it happened, stood beneath a painting of Cornwallis' surrender at Yorktown. When Key Pittman began to introduce his colleagues, senatorial whispers of "She's lovely," "She's charming," arose from those still waiting. The Queen heard these compliments and acknowledged them with a smile. Suspicions and tensions eased, and even the crustiest isolationists melted when the King greeted Senator Ellison D. Smith of South Carolina, whom he had met at the garden party, as "Cotton Ed."

Next, New York's Sol Bloom, acting chairman of the Foreign Affairs Committee, stepped up to present the members of the House. Nervous, he fumbled with his hat and mispronounced his colleagues' names, bumbling the introductions. Following Garner's lead, House members turned on their democratic charm. Robert Mouton, who represented a Creole district in Louisiana, hailed the King and Queen as *"votre majestés"*; then he astounded everyone by grabbing the Queen's hand and kissing it. Nat Patton of Crockett, Texas, accosted the King, shouting: "Cousin George, I bring you greetin's from the far-flung regions of the Empire State of Texas." Turning to a colleague, he stated, "If America can keep Queen Elizabeth, Congress will regard Britain's war debt as cancelled."

Successfully enduring the hot lights and congressional ardor, the King and Queen rushed to the presidential yacht *Potomac* for lunch and a leisurely cruise to Mount Vernon. Here George VI placed a wreath on George Washington's grave. Returning by automobile, the party stopped briefly at the Civilian Conservation Corps camp at nearby Fort Hunt, Virginia. The camp fascinated the King, who wanted to begin a similar operation in Great Britain. Exhausted after a formal dinner at the British Embassy, the King and Queen returned to their train for the trip to Red Bank, New Jersey, where next morning they would board a destroyer, the U.S.S. *Warrington*, and sail to New York City.

On Pier 1 at the Battery a large gray alley cat stretched drowsily on the red carpet intended only for royalty. Policemen shooed away the intruder. Flying the Stars and Stripes aft and the Royal Standard forward, the *Warrington* docked. A bosun piped the King and Queen ashore, where Mayor Fiorello H. La Guardia and Governor Herbert H. Lehman welcomed them. A morning mist hid some skyscrapers from view, but more than three and a half million people turned out to witness the spectacle of royalty. In Central Park a million school children waved British and American flags. But the twenty-five-car motorcade could not linger long in Manhattan. A time schedule had to be kept and security precautions

followed. The motorcycle escort sped up and quickly whisked the King and Queen to the World's Fair in Flushing.

Marines from Quantico, National Guard troops, an eighty-piece band, and more than five hundred guests strained to hear the first sound of the motorcycles. Preparations had been elaborate. The fair planned to give their Majesties a regal welcome, but the guests of honor were already thirty minutes late. The King finally entered Perylon Hall. The large room became silent. Awed by the royal presence, fair officials awaited the King's first words. "When do we eat?" he asked. Grover Whalen, head of the World's Fair, and New York City's official greeter, smilingly ignored the King's question and took him over to a receiving line to meet dignitaries. About half the people had been introduced when the King started to walk away. Whalen heard Ambassador Lindsay say, "His Majesty is leaving now." "He can't do that," Whalen pleaded. La Guardia rushed up to his official greeter. "What the hell are you doing?" he demanded. The King was gone. In less than fifteen minutes he had put a dragging tour back on schedule.

Whalen found the King outside. Defeated at Perylon Hall, he bundled George VI into a car and they drove to the Court of Peace, where the King was to review troops. Precise plans governed the review. As soon as the King stepped into a specially chalked area, a signal would be given and the troops would instantly swing into motion. Whalen was just explaining the chalk mark to the King when their car reached the Court of Peace. George VI, unmindful of Whalen's explanation, shot from the car. Accidentally, he stepped on the chalked spot and the soldiers moved out, much to his surprise. The now puffing Whalen explained. George VI protested: "I won't take the review." Again he demanded, "When do we eat?" Whalen was too out of breath to answer, and the King trotted off. Once more Whalen chugged after him. When he caught up, George VI pleaded, "Where is *it?*" Only then did "Mr. New York" understand, and he directed the King to the nearest rest room.

A few minutes later, while the Meyer Davis orchestra played "Alexander's Ragtime Band" and "Indian Love Call," the King at last ate lunch. Afterward the royal couple toured the fair grounds in a blue and orange trackless train from which emanated strains of "The Sidewalks of New York." The King seemed more at ease in the afternoon, but everyone was relieved when the World's Fair visit ended. George VI and Elizabeth climbed into a waiting automobile for the drive up the Hudson to Hyde Park. There they might rest royal hands swollen from endless handshaking.

True to its isolationist tradition, the Chicago Tribune *ran a cartoon warning Uncle Sam against British pickpockets.*

The Roosevelts were sitting in the library of their Hyde Park mansion when a member of the royal party phoned to explain that they would arrive late. The President had a pitcher of martinis ready when his guests drove in, even though his mother, Sara Delano Roosevelt, insisted that the King would prefer tea. As the King approached the cocktail table, F. D. R. observed, "My mother thinks you should have a cup of tea—she doesn't approve of cocktails." George VI answered, "Neither does my mother," and gratefully took a drink.

The atmosphere at Hyde Park was intimate and informal. Only the butlers gave the gathering any hint of convention, and they inadvertently alleviated that. During the evening meal, a serving table suddenly collapsed, shattering part of the dinner service on the floor. The guilty servant stood in shameful silence, pierced by the stares of the Roosevelt women. He knew that he had overloaded the table, but Mrs. James R. Roosevelt saved him further embarrassment when she said, "I hope none of *my* dishes were broken," and laughed. The King, the Queen, and the President seated themselves in the library after dinner, only to hear a second tinkling crash. Another butler was sprawled on the library floor surrounded by a sea of bottles, glasses, ice cubes, and liquor. The tray of drinks, in the words of Grace Tully, had "hurtled into space" and the butler "bounced after it like a ballplayer sliding into second base." By the time the servant managed to pour the drinks, the hour was late, and everyone soon retired except Roosevelt, George VI, and Mackenzie King.

Left alone, the three men talked more seriously about the perilous drift of events in Europe. The defense of the Caribbean gravely concerned Roosevelt. As early as 1936 he had conceived a plan of establishing bases in Newfoundland, Bermuda, Jamaica, St. Lucia, Antigua, and Trinidad for the better protection of the Americas and to prevent these territories from falling into hostile hands. American naval maneuvers in the winter of 1938–39 had initiated the idea of a Western Atlantic patrol. Roosevelt mentioned that it was a waste of money for Canada to expand her fleet, for the United States could defend the Western Hemisphere. The President also assured his companions that he would try to do something to ease the restrictions of the most recent Neutrality Act. In truth, he explained, he and Hull were doing their best to put public opinion on the right course. Finally, Roosevelt patted the King's knee and said, "Young man, it's time for you to go to bed." George VI went to his room, but before retiring observed to Mackenzie King how impressed he was with Roose-

velt. F. D. R. was like a father, the King said, giving him "his most careful and wise advice."

The next day after church the King spoke with Roosevelt alone and discussed Europe in general terms. The President expressed hope for a Franco-Italian *détente* and was, George VI noted later, "definitely anti-Russian." Returning the conversation to the role of the United States in a future war, F. D. R. promised the King that if American naval patrols spotted a U-boat, they "would sink her at once" and "wait for the consequences." Continuing his promises, Roosevelt declared that if the Germans bombed London, the United States would enter the war. At that point diplomatic discussions ceased; it was time for a picnic.

The Roosevelts wanted to treat their guests to a "traditional" American outing. Mrs. Roosevelt corralled friends to barbecue hot dogs and serve beer. Strawberries for shortcake, a favorite of the King, came from the neighboring farm of Secretary of the Treasury Henry Morgenthau, Jr. The royal couple sampled the hot dogs, but the King's enthusiasm waned when he dropped mustard on his coat. This did not dull his taste for beer, however, and he downed several glasses, blissfully unaware that the Central Women's Christian Temperance Union of Indianapolis had passed a resolution deploring the inclusion of beer on the Hyde Park menu. Princess Te Ata, a half-breed Choctaw-Chickasaw Indian who lived on Park Avenue in New York City, entertained the guests with Indian tales and songs. She was a replacement for the usual Roosevelt picnic game, "musical squat," a scramble for cushions on the lawn rather than for chairs.

Next on the agenda was a swim. The President donned his two-piece bathing suit and the King appeared in a one-piece garment, which James Roosevelt described as a "genuine relic from the era of . . . King Edward VII." Both swimmers piled into F. D. R.'s hand-operated Ford, and the President whizzed the King around Hyde Park; according to James Roosevelt, this gave Scotland Yard palpitations. (The President's Secret Service men, of course, were used to the vehicle.) After a brief dip they joined the others at the house for a quiet supper of fish chowder and oyster crackers.

The visit was over. Like old friends, the Roosevelts and the royal couple exchanged photographs and gifts. They reminisced during the drive to Hyde Park Station, where the King and Queen boarded the train that would take them back to Canada. In parting, George VI assured his hosts, "It's been a long weekend, but a short visit." Dusk covered the valley as the train moved slowly north, and people who had

England's Punch *imagined the mutual surprise of George Washington and George III at the proposed royal visit.*

gathered along the banks of the Hudson began to sing "Auld Lang Syne." Wistfully the Roosevelts returned to Hyde Park.

Certainly the tour had been a personal triumph for George VI and Elizabeth, but it also brought international reverberations. A German editor suggested that the royal visit had been "the most important link in the whole chain of measures whereby Britain has attempted . . . to tie America more firmly to British destinies." Father Charles E. Coughlin, the radio priest from Royal Oak, Michigan, who by that time was rabidly anti-Roosevelt, labelled the tour a bid "to nullify our basic foreign policy of no entanglements." The mystique of monarchy may have captivated many Americans, but cynics saw the visit as only "so much high-grade panhandling," as one of them expressed it. One foreign affairs expert concluded that the British government wanted "to count on North America as a whole for moral and material support in its continental adventures." The deepening of "understanding and sympathy between the English speaking nations," as Roosevelt put it, had aroused a suspicious nerve in the American character.

Although they lacked proof, isolationists had reason for suspicion. Because "America First" sentiment had

for the moment blocked hope of revising neutrality legislation, Roosevelt was seeking a new course that might release United States foreign policy from its legislative fetters. Since Congress had proved recalcitrant, the President believed that personal executive action was necessary. In their conversations George VI had noted that the President was "terribly keen" on naval patrols; yet this was mainly bravado. Roosevelt knew that he could not take a country to war so easily. He had not even thrown his weight behind the Bloom Bill, which remained buried in committee until July. Though Roosevelt's most optimistic statements to the King smacked of active intervention and probably contained the seed of the future "destroyer deal," Lend-Lease, and the "shoot-on-sight" order, in 1939 his interventionism looked to the south and the Caribbean rather than to Europe.

Foremost in the President's mind was defense of the Western Hemisphere. Like most Americans, F. D. R. wished to avoid American participation in a European war, but the former Assistant Secretary of the Navy did not need to be reminded that the Panama Canal and control of the Caribbean were vital to the country's security. The British would have preferred a more positive response toward European problems, but F. D. R. had done little serious thinking beyond hemispheric defense. Only the outbreak of World War II, a few months later, would change that.

Still, the royal visit to the United States constituted an undeniable diplomatic success. The King and Queen had spurred the development of a neighborly spirit between the two countries. Though the visit changed no vote on the proposed revision of neutrality legislation, a better understanding among the Atlantic powers now existed. Americans discovered that royalty went beyond storybook kings and queens. They loved the smiling and personable Elizabeth. Women carefully studied her wardrobe. Men cheered the way George quaffed beer. The King and Queen had sampled good old American hot dogs and liked them. Even the hard-bitten vendors at Coney Island were caught up by the aura of monarchy. The day after the Hyde Park picnic, signs went up on some of the beachside hot-dog stands: "By Special Appointment to his Majesty the King."

Mr. Cantelon is a young scholar and teacher of history currently working on his doctorate at Indiana University.

In addition to many documentary sources at Hyde Park and in Washington, D.C., and contemporary news accounts, the author found particularly interesting John Wheeler-Bennett's biography, King George VI (*St. Martin's, 1958*), Eleanor Roosevelt's This I Remember (*Harper, 1949*), and The Secret Diary of Harold L. Ickes (*Simon & Schuster, 1954*).

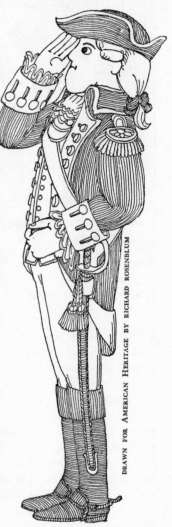

A Cardsharp – or Vice Versa

A soldier in the American army being unfortunately surprised at a game of cards by a sergeant who owed him an old grudge, was carried before the colonel of the regiment, that he might be punished for gaming, against which general orders were very severe. The soldier being asked what he had to say in his defence, replied: That having been religiously educated, and well instructed in the Bible by his parents, and his pay so small that with the greatest economy he had not been able to save enough to buy one, he had therefore purchased an old pack of cards for a few dollars of one of his comrades, which not only served him for a Bible, but made a most excellent almanac besides; then taking out his cards he proceeded thus: "When I see a one, it reminds me that there is but one God; a two, of the Father and Son; a three, of the Father, Son, and Holy Ghost; a four, calls to my remembrance the four evangelists, Matthew, Mark, Luke, and John; a five, the five wise and foolish virgins; a six, that in six days God created the heavens and the earth; a seven, that the seventh was to be kept holy; an eight, of the eight righteous persons that were preserved from the flood, viz.: Noah, his wife, his three sons and their wives; a nine, the nine ungrateful lepers cleansed by our Saviour; a ten, of the Ten Commandments; the queen reminds me of Queen Sheba, who came from the uttermost parts of the earth to hear the wisdom of Solomon; and the king, of the great King of Heaven." The colonel told him he had forgot the knave. "That," replied he, "used to represent Judas; but from this time, when I see the knave, I shall always think of the sergeant who brought me before your honor." . . .

The soldier then continued as follows: "When I count the number of dots on a pack of cards they are three hundred and sixty-five, for so many days there are in a year; when I reckon how many picture cards are in a pack, I find there are twelve, so many months are there in a year; when I reckon how many tricks are won by a pack, I find there are thirteen, this reminds me of the duty I owe to the thirteen United and Independent States of America. Thus they serve both for Bible and almanac." The colonel called his servant, told him to treat the soldier well, and dismissed him, saying he was a very clever fellow.

Reader, be not ashamed of cards, since they may be applied to the best of purposes; the scandal consists not in the use, but in the abuse of them.—*New-Jersey Journal*, December 27, 1780

From Frank Moore's The Diary of the American Revolution, 1775–1781, *edited by John Anthony Scott; Washington Square Press, 1967*

DRAWN FOR AMERICAN HERITAGE BY RICHARD ROSENBLUM